Getting Started with Docker

Weapons-grade learning

April 2024

Nigel Poulton @nigelpoulton

About this edition

This edition was published in April 2024.

I'll update this book at least once per year to make sure you're getting the latest up-to-date info.

Enjoy the book, and get ready to rock 'n' roll with containers!

Nigel Poulton

About the author

Nigel is a technology geek who spends his life diving into cool technologies and creating books and videos that make them easier to learn. He's the author of best-selling books on Docker and Kubernetes, as well as some of the most popular online training videos on the same topics.

Nigel is a Docker Captain, and his latest hyperfixation is WebAssembly on the server (Wasm). Previously, Nigel held senior technology roles at large and small enterprises.

In his free time, he listens to audio books and watches science fiction. He wishes he lived in the future and could explore space-time, the universe, and other mind-bending phenomena. He's passionate about learning, cars, and football (soccer). He lives in England with his fabulous wife and three children.

@nigelpoulton

nigelpoulton.com/books

gsd@nigelpoulton.com

Contents

About the book

This book gets you up-to-speed with Docker and containers fast!

I've carefully chosen the most useful topics and hand-crafted every chapter and example so the book is fun and engaging.

You'll love the book if you're a developer just getting started with containers. You'll also love it if you work in technical marketing, sales, management, architecture, operations, and more.

What does the book cover

The book has seven main chapters packed with theory and hands-on demos.

- **Chapter 1**: Introduces you to the concepts and clarifies important jargon
- **Chapter 2**: Shows you how to get Docker
- **Chapter 3**: Walks you through running your first container
- **Chapter 4**: Containerizes a simple web app
- **Chapter 5**: Goes deeper into images and gets you using Docker Hub
- **Chapter 6**: Deploys and manages a multi-container app
- **Chapter 7**: Introduces you to WebAssembly and demos how Docker and WebAssembly work well together

Will the book make you an expert

No, but it will kick-start your journey to *becoming* an expert.

Will you know what you're talking about when you finish the book

Yes, you'll know **more than enough** to start deploying and managing simple apps with Docker.

Editions

The following English language editions are available from all good book resellers:

- Paperback
- Ebook (including Kindle)

Translations will become available in the near future.

Terminology and responsible language

The book follows guidelines from the Inclusive Naming Initiative[1], which promotes the use of responsible language.

Feedback

If you like the book and it helps your career, share the love by recommending it to a friend and leaving a review on Amazon.

If you spot a typo or want to make a recommendation, email me at **gsd@nigelpoulton.com**.

[1] https://inclusivenaming.org

The sample apps

This is a hands-on book with sample applications.

You can find them on GitHub at:

- **https://github.com/nigelpoulton/gsd-book/**

Don't stress about the apps or GitHub if you're not a developer. The focus of the book is Docker and containers — you do not have to be a GitHub expert, nobody is ;-)

If you already have **git** installed, you can download the apps now with the following command. It's OK if you don't have **git**, we'll show you how to get it and download the apps later in the book.

```
$ git clone https://github.com/nigelpoulton/gsd-book.git
Cloning into 'gsd-book'...
remote: Enumerating objects: 53, done.
remote: Counting objects: 100% (53/53), done.
remote: Compressing objects: 100% (36/36), done.
remote: Total 53 (delta 18), reused 43 (delta 10), pack-reused 0
Receiving objects: 100% (53/53), 52.97 KiB | 986.00 KiB/s, done.
Resolving deltas: 100% (18/18), done.
```

1: Intro to containers

The goal of this chapter is to introduce you to the main concepts and level-set some jargon.

Don't worry if some of this is confusing, we'll cover everything again in more detail later in the book.

I've divided the chapter into the following sections:

- Why containers
- Big picture view
- Images
- Containers
- Registries
- The Open Container Initiative (OCI)
- Containers and virtual machines
- Microservices
- Linux and Windows containers
- The future

Don't run any of the example commands in this chapter. You'll run plenty of commands in future chapters.

Why containers

Before we had containers, we built applications that worked on our laptops and development environments but often failed in production. The main reason was the differences between development and production environments — production would have different versions of libraries and dependencies.

Docker fixed this by standardising the way we *package* and *run* apps.

We're about to find out, but the standard package is the *image,* and the standard way to run is the *container*. The image contains everything the app needs to run.

In short, Docker made sharing and running applications a dream!

Big picture view

Containers are the most popular way to package and run modern applications. They're *smaller, faster,* and more *portable* than virtual machines, and they work with existing applications written in existing languages – no need to learn any new languages or frameworks!

There are two main steps to run an application as a container:

1. Package the app as an *image*
2. Run it as a *container*

The process of packaging an application as an image is called *containerization*. It takes the application source code, including all dependencies, and builds it into an *image*. This image is usually small and contains everything needed to run the app.

Once you have the *image,* you can run it as a *container*.

Under the hood, a container is an *isolated execution environment*. That's jargon for a ring-fenced part of an operating system (OS) dedicated to a single app. Figure 1.1 shows a single OS running four containers. Each container is an isolated part of the OS, each one runs a single app, and none of them knows the others exist.

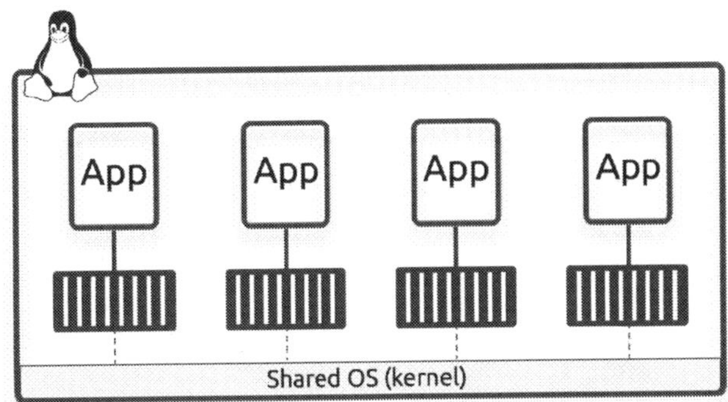

Figure 1.1. Isolated execution environments.

It's common to think of images as *stopped* containers, and containers as *running* images.

Figure 1.2 shows the main steps in taking an application from source code to a running container. The steps are:

1. Develop your app
2. Build the app and dependencies into an image
3. Ship the image to a registry (optional)
4. Run it as a container

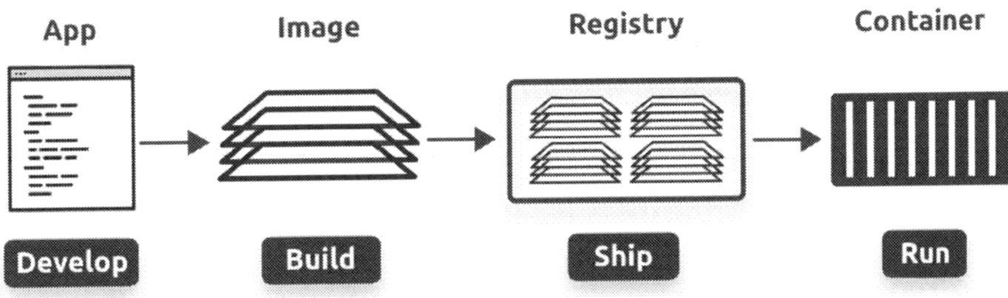

Figure 1.2

The whole process is extremely simple, and we'll walk through it several times in the book.

That's the big picture. Let's dig a bit deeper.

Images

At a high level, an image is a collection of *layers* that comprise the application and all dependencies.

Figure 1.3 shows three layers combined into an image. The bottom layer has a minimal OS and filesystem, the middle layer has the application, and the top layer has dependencies. When stacked together, we call them an image, and they contain everything needed to run the application as a container.

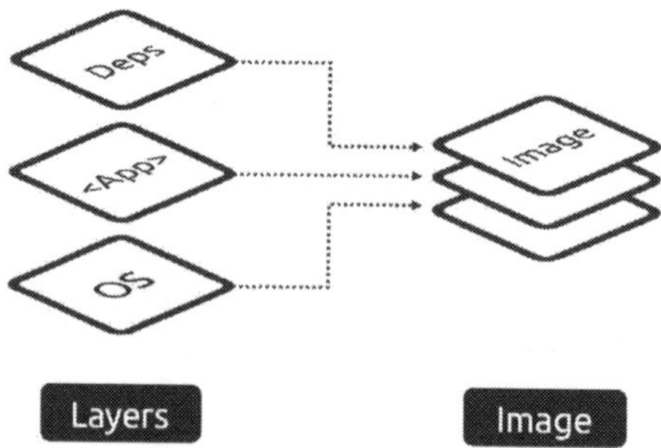

Figure 1.3. Image layering.

The most common way to build an image is with a *Dockerfile* and the `docker build` command. The Dockerfile is a list of instructions that tell `docker build` how to build the image.

The first three lines of the following Dockerfile create the three layers shown in Figure 1.3 (base OS, app, dependencies). The fourth line is metadata telling Docker how to start the app.

```
FROM golang:1.20-alpine         <<==== Start from base OS
COPY go.mod go.sum .            <<==== Copy app and dependencies
RUN go mod download             <<==== Install dependencies
ENTRYPOINT [ "/bin/server" ]  <<==== How to start the app
```

The following command builds a new image called `my-image` using a Dockerfile called `Dockerfile`. Don't run the command, it's just shown here to get you familiar.

```
$ docker build -t my-image . -f Dockerfile
```

The build process starts at the top of the Dockerfile and steps through each instruction in turn:

1. Download the base OS
2. Copy in the app and list of dependencies
3. Install dependencies
4. Record the command to run the app.

Figure 1.4 shows a simplified version of the Dockerfile and its relationship to the image layers. Each of the three lines in the Dockerfile refers to a different layer in the image.

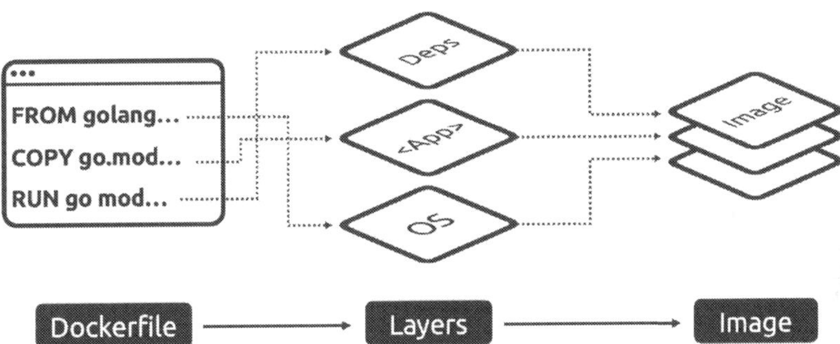

Figure 1.4. Dockerfiles and images.

The terms, *container image, Docker image,* and *OCI image* all mean the same thing. Usually, we just call them *images*.

Containers

Images are used to start one or more containers.

Figure 1.5 shows three identical containers started from a single image.

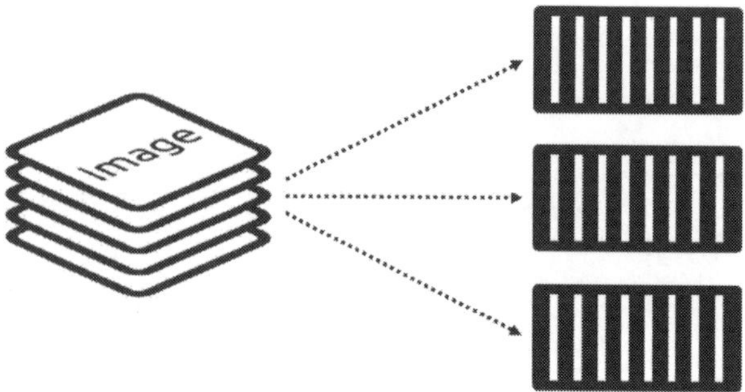

Figure 1.5. Single image starting three containers.

If you're a developer, think of images and containers as similar to classes and objects — we create containers from images in a similar way to creating objects from classes. If you're more of a sysadmin or DevOps, it might be helpful to think of them as similar to VM templates and running VMs — we create containers from images in a similar way to creating VMs from VM templates.

The following example command starts a new container called *web* from an image called *my-image.*

```
$ docker run --name web my-image
```

Registries

Container registries are centralised places to store and retrieve images. Sometimes we call them *container registries, Docker registries,* or *OCI registries*.

The acts of storing and retrieving images are called *pushing* and *pulling*. For example, you *push* an image **to** a registry, and you *pull* an image **from** a registry.

The following command shows an image being *pushed* to GitHub Container Registry.

```
$ docker push ghcr.io/nigelpoulton/gsd-book:web
c41833b44d91: Pushed
170db43947cc: Pushed
<Snip>
a7d0e2584121: Pushed
```

The next command shows an image being *pulled* from Docker Hub.

```
$ docker pull docker.io/nigelpoulton/gsd-book:web
web: Pulling from nigelpoulton/gsd-book
63b65145d645: Pull complete
<Snip>
55d7c29dff3f: Pull complete
Digest: sha256:3b497b2cc153ee8c4ccc...1c8c1b72a27efd
docker.io/nigelpoulton/gsd-book:web
```

Figure 1.6 shows pushing and pulling an image to a registry.

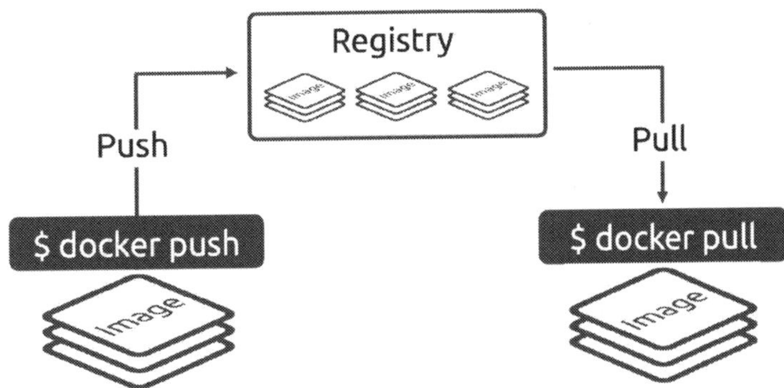

Figure 1.6. Pushing and pulling images.

Most registries provide additional features such as access controls, vulnerability scanning, and integration with automated build pipelines.

That's the fundamentals of images, containers, and registries. Don't worry if some of it still needs to be clarified, there's plenty of hands-on and more explanations later in the book.

The Open Container Initiative

The Open Container Initiative (OCI)[2] is a governance body responsible for developing and maintaining the core standards that have enabled the container ecosystem to thrive.

It currently maintains three specifications:

- Image spec
- Runtime spec
- Distribution spec

The *image spec* defines standards around image format, such as structure, contents, and metadata.

The *runtime spec* defines how images should be unpacked and executed as containers.

The *distribution spec* standardises the distribution of container images via registries.

We often compare these standards to the standardisation of rail tracks. For example, having rail tracks with a standard gauge of 1,435mm (4 ft 8.5 in) fueled the expansion of railways by giving train builders the confidence their trains would work on any track using the standard gauge. The OCI standards have similarly enabled the container ecosystem to expand and thrive.

Each of the following terms means the same thing:

- **Image:** *container image, Docker image, OCI image*
- **Container:** *Docker container, Linux container, OCI container*
- **Registry:** *container registry, Docker registry, OCI registry*

All of the technologies and examples in this book implement the OCI standards.

[2] https://opencontainers.org

Containers and virtual machines

It's common to compare containers with virtual machines — both are popular ways of *packaging* applications and are both forms of *virtualisation*:

On the packaging front, containers are smaller, faster, and more portable than virtual machines (VM).

On the virtualisation front, VMs virtualise hardware, whereas containers virtualise operating systems (OS). For example:

- Every VM looks, smells, and feels exactly like a physical server
- Every container looks, smells, and feels exactly like a regular OS

Figure 1.7 shows a shared host with hardware and an OS in the middle. It also shows VM virtualisation on the left and container virtualisation on the right. The VMs on the left share and virtualise the same hardware, whereas the containers on the right share and virtualise the same OS.

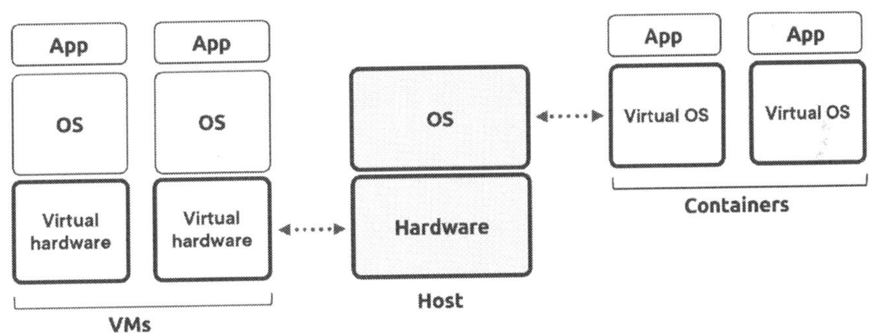

Figure 1.7. Comparing container and VM virtualisation.

A major advantage of the container model is the shared OS.

For example, you need three operating systems to run the two apps on the left of Figure 1.7. These include the OS on the shared host in the middle, plus one for each of the two VMs. Each one is a full-blown OS that consumes CPU, memory, and disk space. In contrast, the container model only needs the shared OS of the host in the middle.

This means any hardware can run a lot more containers than VMs.

It's also common to run containers on top of virtual machines. Most setups like this run multiple containers per VM. Figure 1.8 shows two VMs on the same host, each running multiple containers.

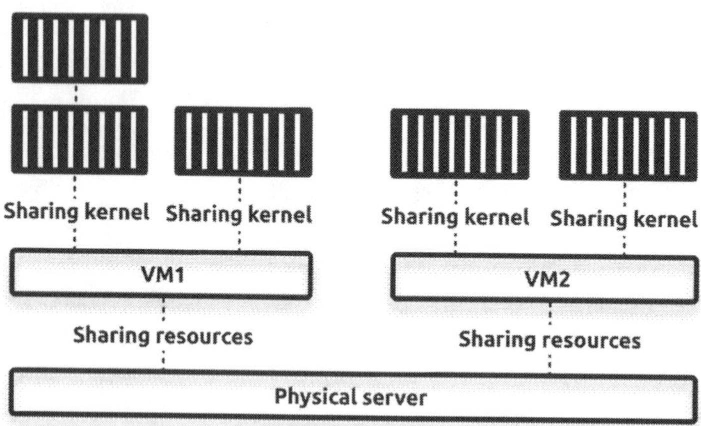

Figure 1.8. Containers on top of VMs.

In summary, containers virtualise operating systems and are smaller, faster, and more portable than VMs. This means any infrastructure can run more containers than VMs.

Microservices

Before containers, we built *monolithic applications*. This is jargon for an application where every feature is developed, deployed, and managed as a single complex app.

Figure 1.9 shows a monolithic app with six features. All six features are developed, compiled, deployed, and managed as a single object.

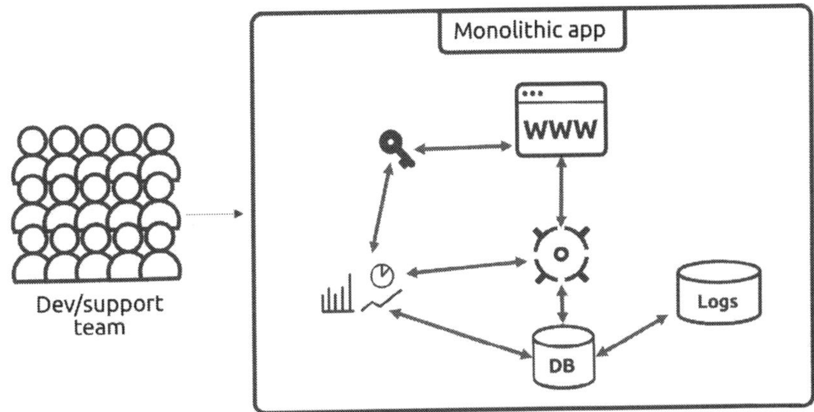

Figure 1.9. Monolithic app

Apps like this have the following challenges:

- They're complex and hard to develop
- Updates and fixes are high risk
- Scaling is imprecise

Consider a couple of quick examples.

Patching a monolithic app's *reporting* feature involves taking the entire application down, patching the whole thing, and then carefully bringing it all back up. It would be much easier if the *reporting* feature wasn't built into the overall app, and you could patch or update it independently.

As another example, imagine it's year-end and everyone's running end-of-year reports. There's no way to scale just the *reporting* feature of a monolithic app. The only option is to scale the entire application by moving everything to more powerful servers or VMs. It would be much easier if the *reporting* feature wasn't built into the overall app, and you could scale it independently.

Enter microservices…

Microservices is a modern design pattern where every application *feature* is developed, deployed, and managed as its own small independent application.

As an example, converting the application in Figure 1.9 to a microservices app would require all six features to be developed, deployed, and managed as six *small applications*. This is actually where the term *microservice* comes from:

- Small (micro)
- Application (service)

Figure 1.10 shows the same application redesigned as a *microservices application.* Each microservice is built as its own image and deployed as its own container. Each can have its own small development team, and each is loosely coupled with the other microservices over the IP network. Importantly, each microservice can be updated and scaled independently. Scaling is done by adding and removing containers.

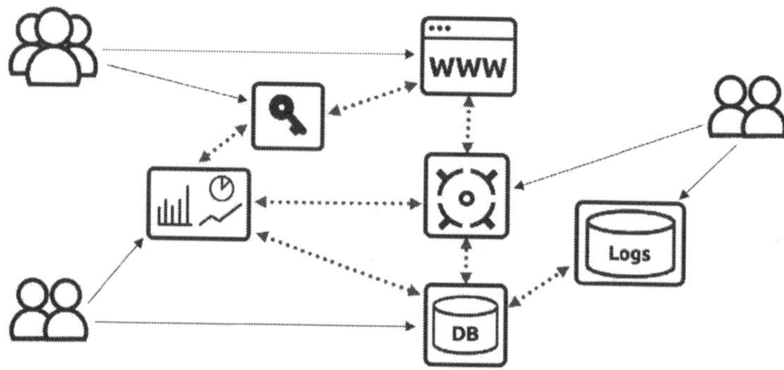

Figure 1.10. Microservices app

Despite these architectural differences, users interact with the app in the same way and get the same outputs. So, from a user perspective, the app is no different.

In summary, microservices is a design pattern where individual application features are developed, deployed, and managed as small independent apps running as containers. These communicate over the network and provide users with the same *application experience.* It makes it possible to independently patch, update, and scale specific parts of the app.

Linux containers and Windows containers

Docker supports Linux and Windows containers.

As shown in Figure 1.11, Linux containers run Linux apps on Linux hosts, whereas Windows containers run Windows apps on Windows hosts.

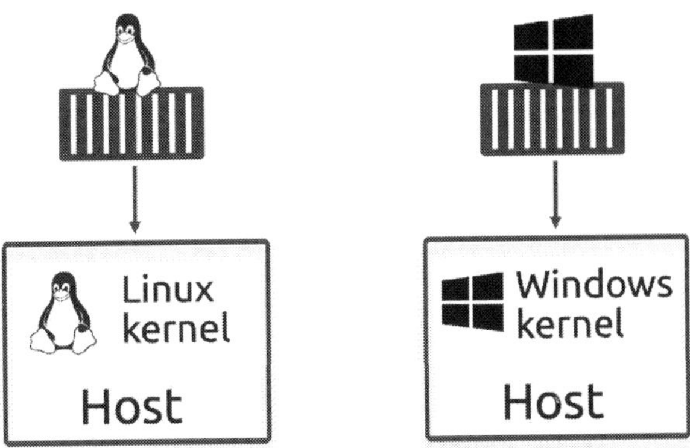

Figure 1.11. Linux and Windows containers

The exception to this rule is Windows hosts with *WSL 2* installed. WSL 2 is the *Windows Subsystem for Linux* and provides a Linux kernel on Windows hosts. These hosts can run Windows **and** Linux containers.

Despite this, the vast majority of containers are Linux, and you rarely see Windows containers.

The future

Containers are the go-to solution for most modern applications, and the ecosystem is growing fast. However, WebAssembly is already powering a new wave of cloud computing, and containers are evolving to play an important role. We cover WebAssembly and containers in a later chapter.

The point is, containers will continue to play a huge role in the future of cloud computing.

Jargon recap

This section recaps the main jargon from the chapter.

OCI. The OCI is the Open Container Initiative. It's a lightweight governance body that creates and maintains standards for low-level container technologies such as images, runtimes, and registries. Docker creates OCI-compliant images, implements an OCI-compliant runtime, and Docker Hub is an OCI-compliant registry.

Image. Images contain a single application, all required dependencies, and the metadata required to start the application as a container. We sometimes call them *OCI images, container images,* or *Docker images*.

Container. A container is an isolated part of an OS designed to run a single application. To an application, a container looks exactly like a regular OS. Containers are smaller, faster, and more portable than virtual machines.

Registry. A registry is a centralised place for storing and retrieving images. We sometimes call them *OCI registries,* and storing and retrieving images is called *pushing* and *pulling*.

Host. Every container executes on a *host*. The host can be a physical server or a virtual machine and can be Linux or Windows. The host provides the operating system that is shared by every running container. For example, 10 containers on the same host all share the host's operating system kernel.

Kernel. A kernel is the core features and functions of an operating system. We sometimes use the terms *kernel* and *operating system* interchangeably.

Microservices. Microservices is a design pattern for modern applications where every feature is developed, deployed, and managed as its own small application (microservice). Each microservice is deployed as a container, enabling frequent updates and precise scaling.

Linux container. Linux containers execute Linux applications and must run on a host with a Linux kernel. This can be a Windows host running the WSL 2 backend.

Windows container. Windows containers execute Windows applications and must run on a Windows host.

WSL 2. WSL is the Windows Subsystem for Linux and allows Linux containers to be developed and executed on Windows hosts.

Figure 1.12 should help you remember some of the jargon.

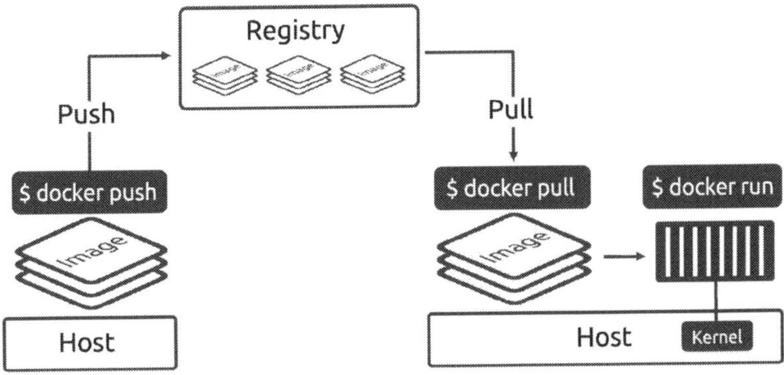

Figure 1.12

Chapter summary

In this chapter, you learned that containers are the most popular way of running modern applications. You also learned that containers are smaller, faster, and more portable than virtual machines.

Containerization is the process of packaging an application and all its dependencies into a container image. We normally store images in registries for easy access.

Running a container usually involves *pulling* its image from a registry and starting the container from the image. You can create multiple containers from a single image.

Microservices is a way to develop, deploy, and manage complex applications as a set of smaller applications. Each of these small applications is called a *microservice*, and they communicate over the network to form a useful application that can be easily updated and scaled.

Linux and Windows apps can both be containerized. Linux apps require a host with a Linux kernel, and Windows apps require a host with a Windows kernel. Almost all containers are Linux containers.

Finally, you learned that containers already work with WebAssembly and are positioned well to play an even bigger role in the future of cloud computing.

2: Getting Docker

Lots of tools exist that allow you to build and run OCI containers. However, this is a getting started book, so we'll focus on two of the easiest:

- Docker Desktop
- Multipass

We'll also show you how to get a Docker Account (they're free) and how to install the Git command line tool so you can download the sample apps.

The chapter is divided as follows:

- Docker Desktop
- Multipass
- Docker Hub and Docker accounts
- Install the git CLI

Docker Desktop

Docker Desktop is the best way to work with Docker. It's simple to install, has a great UI, and you get the full Docker experience.

If you install Docker Desktop, you can follow along with every example without any extra effort.

Figure 2.1 shows the *Containers* tab of Docker Desktop. It shows a single container and provides simple buttons to start, stop, delete, and more. On the left, it has tabs for image management, volume management, vulnerability management (Docker Scout), and working with builds. There's also a thriving marketplace for extensions.

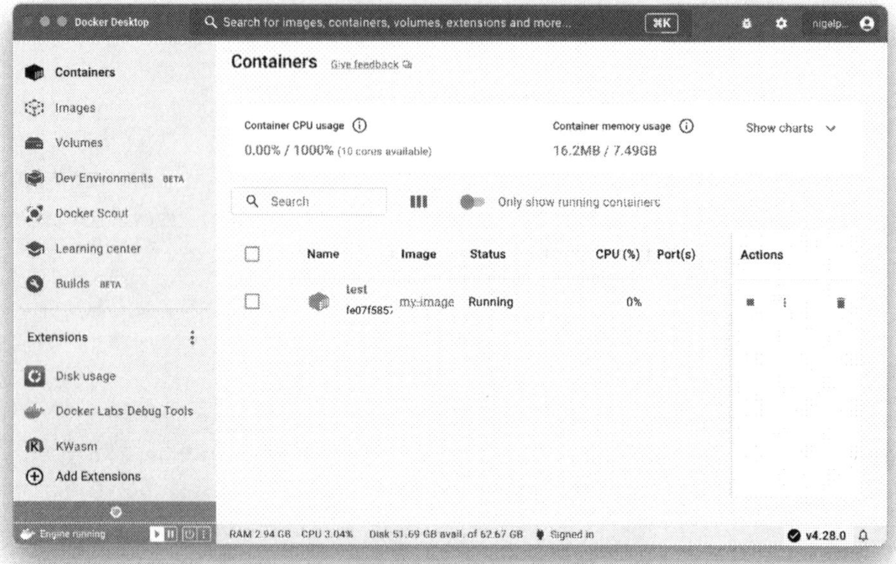

Figure 2.1. Docker Desktop UI

A quick word on Docker Desktop licensing…

Using Docker Desktop for personal use is free. However, you have to pay to use it for work if your company has more than 250 employees or does more than $10M (USD) in annual revenue.

Installing and testing Docker Desktop

Installing Docker Desktop is as simple as:

1. Searching the web for *Docker Desktop*
2. Downloading the installer for your system
3. Firing up the installer and following the next, next, next instructions

Windows users should install the WSL 2 subsystem when prompted.

After the installation completes, you may need to start the app manually. Mac users get a whale icon in the menu bar at the top when it's running, whereas Windows users get it in the system tray at the bottom. Clicking the whale exposes some basic controls and lets you open the GUI. It also shows whether Docker Desktop is running.

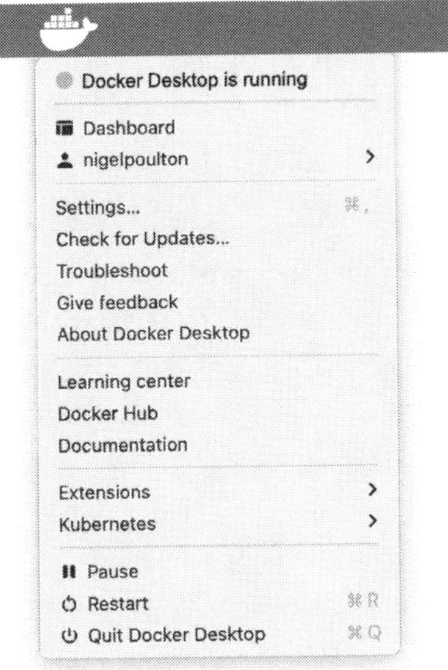

Figure 2.2

Windows users will have an additional option to switch between *Linux containers* and *Windows containers*. You need to switch to Linux containers to follow the examples.

Open a command line and type some commands to see if Docker is installed and working.

```
$ docker --version
Docker version 26.0.0, build 2ae903e

$ docker compose version
Docker Compose version v2.25.0
```

Congratulations, Docker Desktop is installed, and you have a full Docker development environment that you can use to follow along with the examples.

Multipass

Multipass is a free tool for Linux, Mac, and Windows that makes creating virtual machines running Docker easy. It's not as easy to use as Docker Desktop and doesn't have all the same features. For example, you don't get a slick GUI or vulnerability scanning.

If you have Docker Desktop, you do not need Multipass.

If you cannot install Docker Desktop, Multipass will allow you to follow along with ***most*** of the examples in the book. Some of the examples may only work with Docker Desktop. This is because Docker Desktop gets new features first.

Installing and testing Multipass

Go to `https://multipass.run/install` and install the right edition for your system.

Once installed, open a command line and run the following command to create a new VM called **gsd-vm** ("gsd" is short for getting started with docker). The command uses the **docker** template to create a VM with Docker already installed.

```
$ multipass launch docker --name gsd-vm
```

It'll take a minute or two to download the template and launch the VM.

List VMs to make sure it launched properly.

```
$ multipass ls
Name            State        IPv4              Image
gsd-vm          Running      192.168.64.37     Ubuntu 22.04 LTS
                             172.17.0.1
                             172.18.0.1
```

Make a note of the VM's **192** IP address, as you'll need this for the examples later in the book.

Run a `multipass shell gsd-vm` command to connect to the VM, and then run some `docker` commands to verify the installation.

You can type `exit` at any time to come out of the VM and return to your local machine. Likewise, you can type `multipass shell gsd-vm` to get back to the VM.

Docker Hub and Docker accounts

Some of the examples later in the book will push images to Docker Hub.

Other registries exist, and you can use those. However, if you don't already have an account with another registry, I recommend you start with Docker Hub — it's easy to use, and the interface and API have been very stable for a very long time.

Go to `hub.docker.com` and click the **Sign up** button. This will take you to the sign-up page, where you can register for a free account.

Once you have an account, you can sign into it with Docker Desktop. This will seamlessly sign you into Docker Hub as well. If you're not using Docker Desktop, run the `docker login` command from your host or VM with Docker installed.

Install the git CLI

The source code and config files for the sample apps are hosted on GitHub.

The easiest way to get them is to *clone* them with the `git` command line tool.

Don't worry if you don't know how to use Git, nobody does ;-)

Search the web for *install git cli* and follow the instructions for your system.

Once it's installed, run the following command. It will create a `gsd-book` directory containing all the files you need to follow along.

```
$ git clone https://github.com/nigelpoulton/gsd-book.git
```

Chapter summary

In this chapter, you saw two easy ways to get a Docker development environment.

Docker Desktop is the best way to work with Docker on your laptop or personal computer. It provides a slick UI and a wide range of powerful features. It's free to use for personal projects and personal learning. However, if you want to use it for work, and your company has more than 250 employees or does more than $10M in annual revenue, you have to pay for a license.

Multipass is another way to get a local Docker environment. It spins up a lightweight VM with the Docker engine installed. However, it doesn't have all the features of Docker Desktop and it may not work for all the examples.

You also learned that *Docker Personal* accounts are free, and they get you access to Docker Hub.

There are lots of other tools that let you build and manage containers.

3: Running your first container

This chapter walks you through creating, stopping, restarting, and deleting your first container. It's a really simple example and won't take you long. However, it's a great way to get some hands-on experience, and it'll reinforce a lot of the things you learned in the previous chapters.

Later chapters will cover more interesting examples.

I've split the chapter as follows:

- Pre-reqs
- Running your first container
- Managing containers with Docker Desktop

Pre-reqs

You'll need a Docker environment to follow along. The previous chapter showed you how to install Docker Desktop and Multipass.

Open a new command line if you're following along with Docker Desktop.

If you're following along with Multipass, open a command line and run the following command to log on to your Docker VM. The command assumes your VM is called `gsd-vm`.

```
$ multipass shell gsd-vm
```

Running your first container

You're about to complete all of the following steps:

- Check for existing containers and images
- Run your first container
- Check the container and image
- Stop, restart, and delete the container

Check for existing containers and images

The purpose of this section is to confirm you're on a clean system with no pre-existing containers or images. If you're following along on Multipass, you may have a pre-existing Portainer container and image. That's OK.

Run a `docker ps` command to list any running containers.

```
$ docker ps
CONTAINER ID   IMAGE     COMMAND    STATUS    PORTS     NAMES
```

The output shows no containers.

Now run a `docker images` to see a list of local images.

```
$ docker images
REPOSITORY   TAG       IMAGE ID   CREATED   SIZE
```

The output shows no images.

You're on a clean system. Let's run your first container.

Run your first container

Run the following command to create a new container called `test`.

```
$ docker run -d --name test -p 5555:8080 nigelpoulton/gsd-book

Unable to find image 'nigelpoulton/gsd-book:latest' locally
latest: Pulling from nigelpoulton/gsd-book
ee605d576664: Download complete
4f4fb700ef54: Download complete
53062d7cc4ed: Download complete
bdb2de7ba06c: Download complete
56b352bc4d6a: Download complete
Digest: sha256:262ad15072366133dc...7290cef95634f237556056
Status: Downloaded newer image for nigelpoulton/gsd-book:latest
f879f4b0571022dad8197be14db222ef75b5280f4b02a804632d30b8381bb88d
```

Congratulations, you just created your first container!

However, before testing it, let's look at what happened.

`docker run` is the command to start a new container.

The `-d` flag makes sure the container starts in the background (detached) and doesn't lock up your terminal.

The `-p 5555:8080` option maps port `5555` on your Docker host to port `8080` inside the container. There's a lot going on here, so let's unpack it.

The container runs a web server listening on port `8080`. Mapping this to port `5555` on the host means we can open a browser on that port and connect to the app in the container. Figure 3.1 shows the Docker host running the container on port `8080`. This is mapped to port `5555` on the host, and a browser on the host connects to port `5555`.

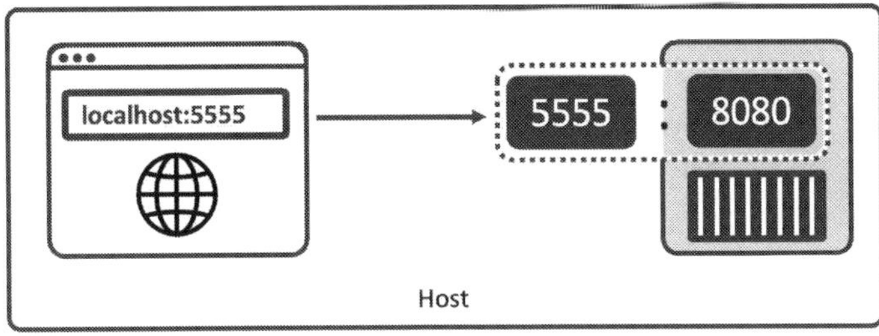

Figure 3.1. Container port mappings.

The last argument, `nigelpoulton/gsd-book`, is the name of the image to start the container from.

A lot of things happened when you hit `Return`. We'll show the output again for reference:

```
Unable to find image 'nigelpoulton/gsd-book:latest' locally
latest: Pulling from nigelpoulton/gsd-book
ee605d576664: Download complete
4f4fb700ef54: Download complete
53062d7cc4ed: Download complete
bdb2de7ba06c: Download complete
56b352bc4d6a: Download complete
Digest: sha256:262ad15072366133dc...7290cef95634f237556056
Status: Downloaded newer image for nigelpoulton/gsd-book:latest
f879f4b0571022dad8197be14db222ef75b5280f4b02a804632d30b8381bb88d
```

The first line shows Docker looking for a local copy of the image and not finding one. As a result, it searched Docker Hub for an image called `nigelpoulton/gsd-docker`, found it, and pulled it. Remember, the term for downloading an image is *pulling*.

The next few lines show Docker *pulling* all five image layers.

The last three lines show the image digest, a success message, and the ID of the container that just started.

Now that we know what happened, let's connect to the app and test it works.

If you're using Docker Desktop, open a browser to `http://localhost:5555/`.

If you're using Multipass, open a browser to port `5555` on your Multipass VM's **192** IP address. You can find this IP address by typing `ip a | grep 192` inside the VM, or by running the `multipass list` command from outside the VM.

Figure 3.2 shows the working app.

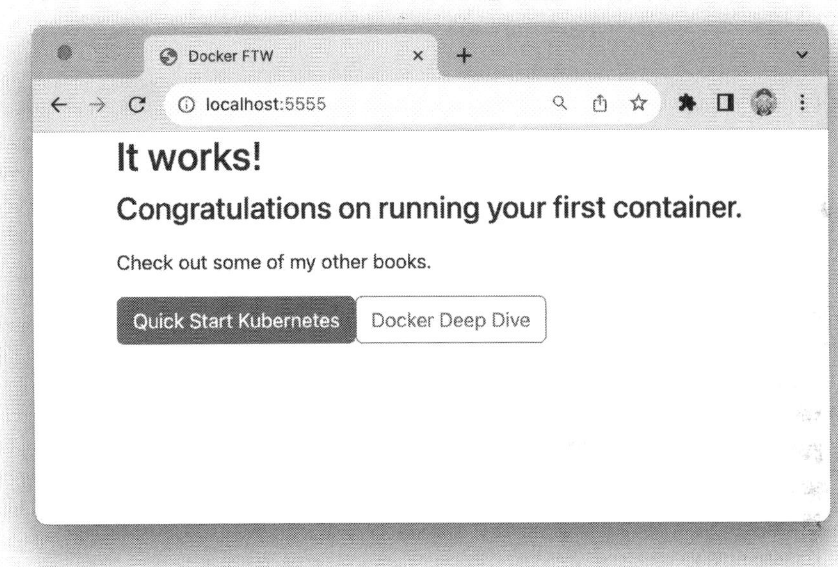

Figure 3.2. The working app.

The app is working!

You just used `docker run` to start a new container. This pulled an image from Docker Hub and unpacked the app into a new container. It also exposed the app on your local machine, and you used a browser to connect to it.

Check the container and image

Run another `docker ps` to see the running container. The output is trimmed to fit the page, but you can see the container is called **test**, it's based on the correct image, and it's mapping port `5555` to `8080`.

```
$ docker ps
CTR ID    IMAGE                    ...  PORTS                  NAMES
f89..710  nigelpoulton/gsd-book    ...  0.0.0.0:5555->8080     test
```

Now, check for local images.

```
$ docker images
REPOSITORY             TAG      IMAGE ID    CREATED     SIZE
nigelpoulton/gsd-book  latest   262...236   5 min ago   111MB
```

You now have a local copy of the `nigelpoulton/gsd-book` image. Remember, the `docker run` command couldn't find a local copy of the image, so it pulled a copy from Docker Hub.

Stop, restart, and delete the container

It's easy to stop and start containers.

Stop the container with the following command. It may take a few seconds while Docker gives the app 10 seconds to exit gracefully.

```
$ docker stop test
test
```

If you go back to your browser and refresh the page, it won't work. This is because you stopped the app.

Restart it.

```
$ docker start test
test
```

The app is back up, and refreshing your browser will work.

Delete the container with the following command. The `-f` flag forces the operation and doesn't give the app the usual 10-second grace period.

```
$ docker rm test -f
test
```

The container is deleted, and refreshing your browser will fail. However, you still have a local copy of the image.

```
$ docker images
REPOSITORY              TAG       IMAGE ID    CREATED     SIZE
nigelpoulton/gsd-book   latest    262...236   9 min ago   111MB
```

Congratulations. You created a container, stopped it, restarted it, and deleted it. Now, let's see how to do it with the Docker Desktop GUI.

Managing containers with Docker Desktop

You'll need Docker Desktop to follow along with these steps.

Docker Desktop is under active development, and UI features are subject to change. I'll work hard to keep the screenshots and instructions up-to-date. However, don't worry if the UI looks slightly different; the overall workflow and results will be the same.

If you've been following along, you'll have a single local image and no containers.

Click the Docker whale in your menu bar or system tray, and choose the **Dashboard** option. This will open Docker Desktop in the **Containers** view.

At the time of writing, there's no way to start a new container from this view.

Switch to the **Images** view, where you should see the `nigelpoulton/gsd-book` image pulled in the previous steps. Click the play/run triangle to the right of the image in the **Actions** column. This will open the *Run a new container* box, as shown in Figure 3.3. Expand the **Optional settings** and fill out the form as shown.

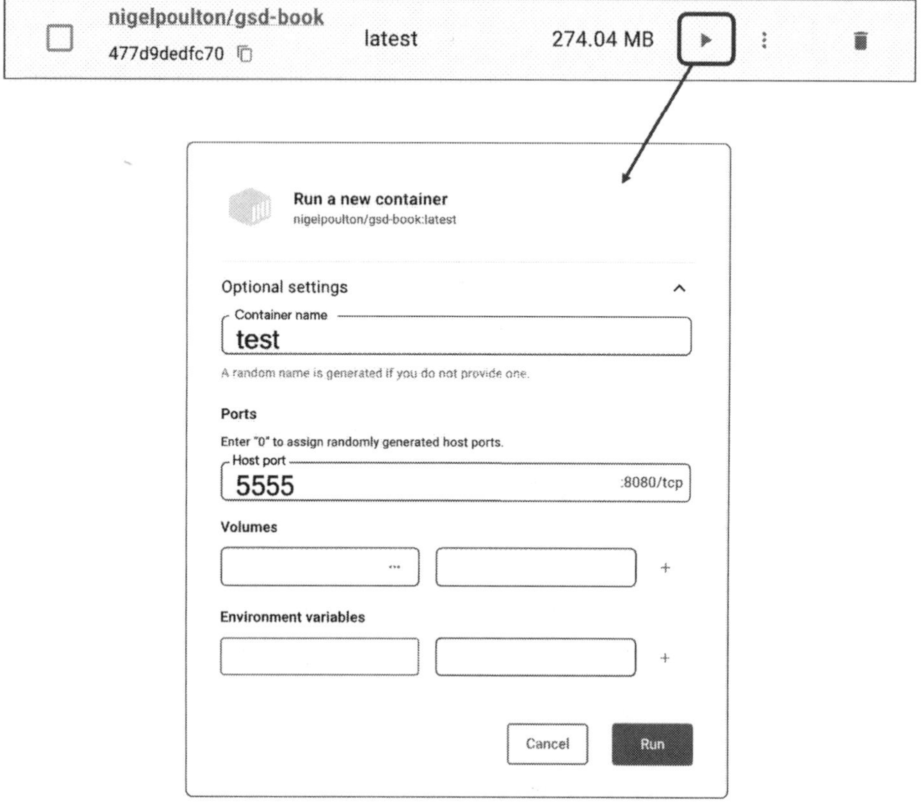

Figure 3.3. Running a new container in Docker Desktop.

Click the big blue **Run** button and then switch back to the **Containers** tab to see the running container.

You get a summary view of the container that's similar to the `docker ps` command. Feel free to filter which columns are shown.

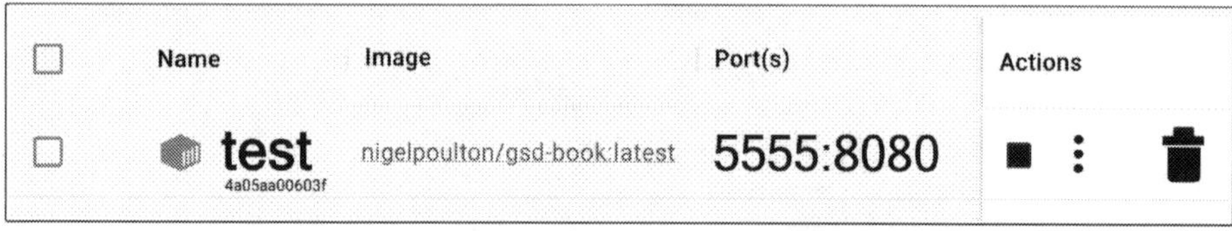

Figure 3.4. Containers view in Docker Desktop.

The **Actions** column on the far right has buttons to stop and delete the container. You can also expand the three dots to see more actions.

Clicking the container's name brings up a new screen that lets you inspect logs, inspect the container's config, browse the container's filesystem, run commands from an exec session, and more. It even gives you simple buttons to control *stopping, restarting,* and *deleting.*

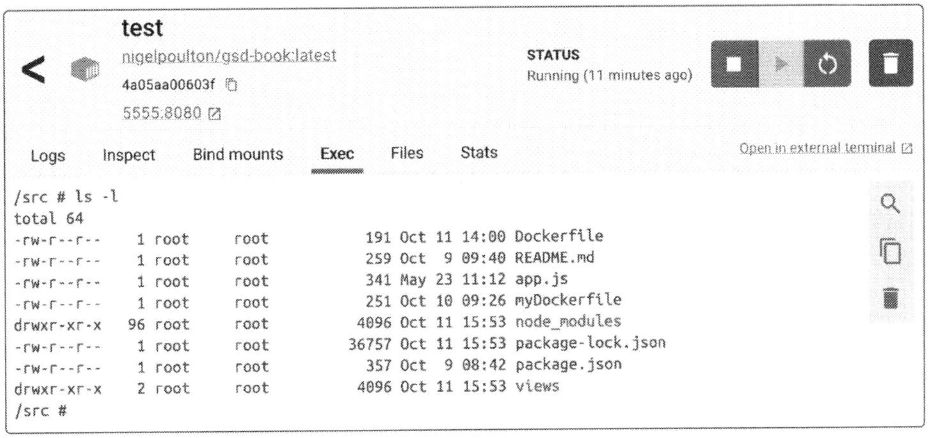
test
nigelpoulton/gsd-book:latest
4a05aa00603f
5555:8080
STATUS
Running (11 minutes ago)
Logs
Inspect
Bind mounts
Exec
Files
Stats
Open in external terminal
/src # ls -l
total 64
-rw-r--r-- 1 root root 191 Oct 11 14:00 Dockerfile
-rw-r--r-- 1 root root 259 Oct 9 09:40 README.md
-rw-r--r-- 1 root root 341 May 23 11:12 app.js
-rw-r--r-- 1 root root 251 Oct 10 09:26 myDockerfile
drwxr-xr-x 96 root root 4096 Oct 11 15:53 node_modules
-rw-r--r-- 1 root root 36757 Oct 11 15:53 package-lock.json
-rw-r--r-- 1 root root 357 Oct 9 08:42 package.json
drwxr-xr-x 2 root root 4096 Oct 11 15:53 views
/src #

Figure 3.5. Detailed container view in Docker Desktop.

Click the back button (<) at the top left to return to the main `Container` screen.

Clicking on the image name in the **Image** column takes you to a view of the image layers and a detailed report on vulnerabilities (Figure 3.6). You even get a drop-down with recommended fixes. This is a very powerful screen, but it's beyond the scope of a getting started book.

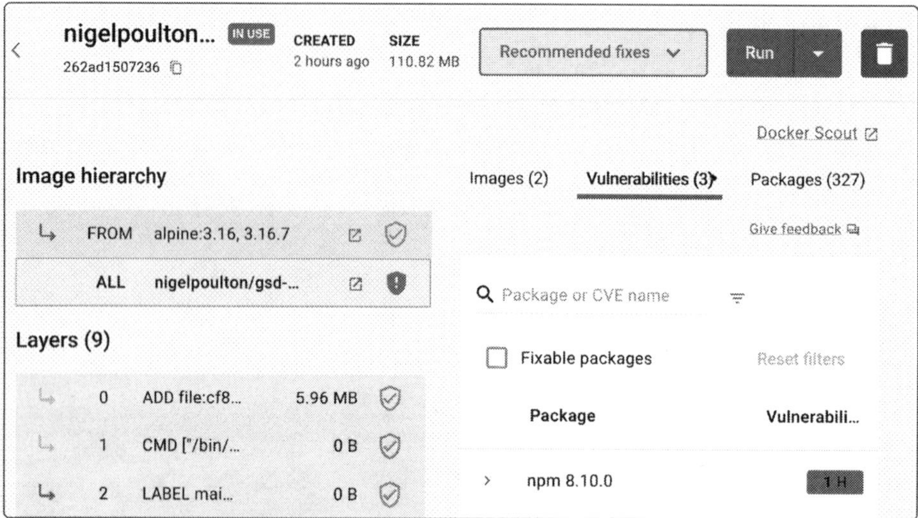

Figure 3.6. View of image and vulnerabilities.

Back at the main **Container** view, the **Ports** column offers an easy way to launch the app in a browser. If you click the port mapping, you'll see the same app as before.

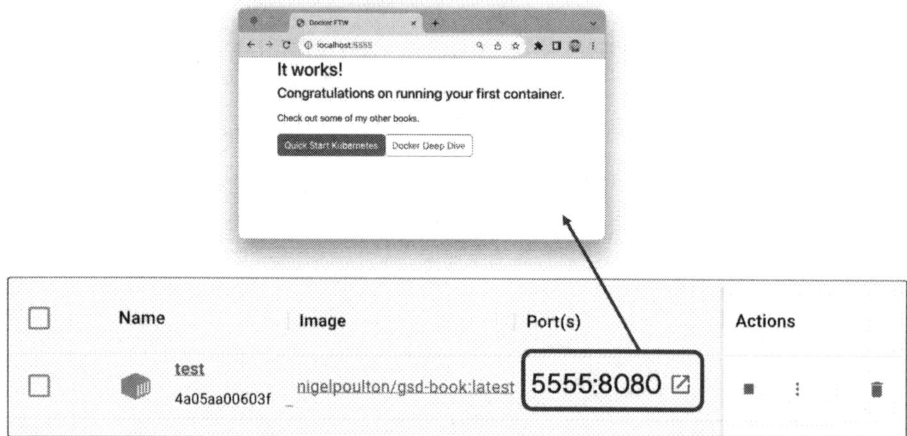

Figure 3.7. Testing the app with Docker Desktop.

Let's use Docker Desktop to stop and delete the container, and then delete the image.

From the **Containers** page, stop the container by clicking the stop square to the right of the container under the **Actions** column. Give it 10 seconds until the container icon turns grey, indicating the container is stopped.

Now click the trash can icon (delete) under the **Actions** column and click **Delete forever** when the warning box appears.

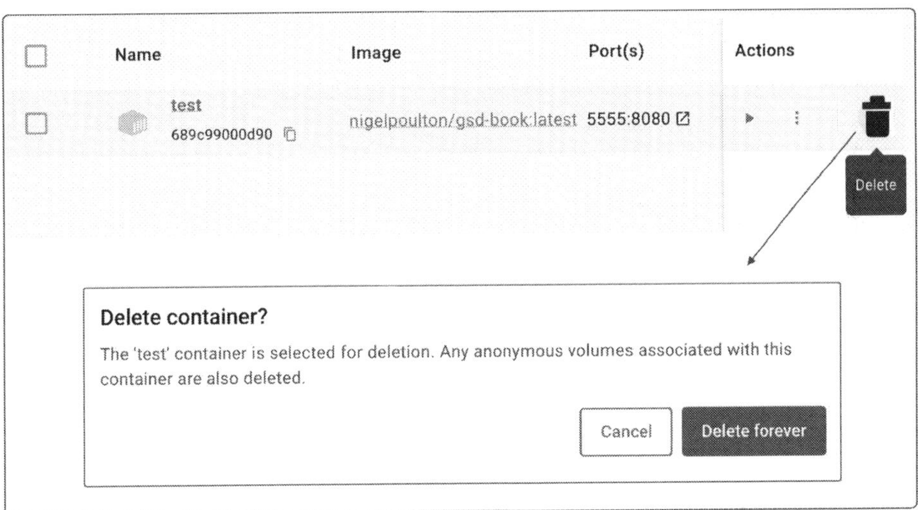

Figure 3.8. Deleting a container in Docker Desktop.

The **Containers** view is now empty, and the container no longer exists.

Switch to the **Images** view and do the same — click the trash can icon (delete) under the **Actions** column and click **Delete forever** when prompted.

The container and image are now deleted from your system. Feel free to switch to the command line and run a `docker ps` and `docker images` to check.

We've only scratched the surface of what's available in Docker Desktop. We'll explore more in later chapters.

Chapter summary

In this chapter, you ran your first container!

You deployed it with `docker run`. This *pulled* an image from Docker Hub, unpacked the app into a new container, and executed it.

While it was running, you used `docker ps` and `docker images` to view the running container and see the image it was based on. You also used other `docker` commands to stop, start, and delete a container.

You then used Docker Desktop to do most of it through the slick UI.

4: Containerizing an application

Docker is all about the apps!

In this chapter, we'll *containerize* a Node.js app and run it in a container.

You do not need to be a Node.js developer.

We'll divide the chapter as follows:

- Pre-reqs
- Overview of the app
- Test the app
- Containerize the app
- Test the containerized app

Pre-reqs

You'll need all of the following if you plan on following along:

- An up-to-date Docker environment
- A clone of the book's GitHub repo
- Node.js (optional)

This chapter uses the new **docker init** command which is only available on Docker Desktop. Don't worry though, I've included a copy of the Dockerfile in the GitHub repo so that you can follow along if you don't have Docker Desktop. I'll explain what to do when the time comes.

You'll also need a clone of the book's GitHub repo, which is jargon for downloading a copy of the files required to build the app. If you don't have the **git** CLI installed, search the web for instructions on how to install it on your system.

Once you have **git** installed, open a terminal and run the following command to clone the repo. This will copy the app files into a new directory called `gsd-book`.

```
$ git clone https://github.com/nigelpoulton/gsd-book.git
Cloning into 'gsd-book'...
remote: Enumerating objects: 8, done.
remote: Counting objects: 100% (8/8), done.
remote: Compressing objects: 100% (6/6), done.
remote: Total 8 (delta 0), reused 8 (delta 0), pack-reused 0
Receiving objects: 100% (8/8), 11.51 KiB | 310.00 KiB/s, done.
```

Run the following commands to change into the `gsd-book/node-app` directory and check the files are present.

```
$ cd gsd-book/node-app

$ ls -l
-rw-r--r--  1 nigelpoulton  staff    341  app.js
-rw-r--r--  1 nigelpoulton  staff  36757  package-lock.json
-rw-r--r--  1 nigelpoulton  staff    357  package.json
drwxr-xr-x  3 nigelpoulton  staff     96  views
-rw-r--r--  1 nigelpoulton  staff   1686  sample-compose.yaml
-rw-r--r--  1 nigelpoulton  staff   1174  sample-Dockerfile
```

You now have everything needed to follow along.

Overview of the app

This section walks you through the sample app and explains how it works. You do **not** need to be a Node expert or a JavaScript developer to follow along. I'm not a Node expert or a JS developer!

The app is only four files. If you followed the previous steps, you'll have copies on your local machine.

- app.js
- views/
- package.json
- package-lock.json

The `app.js` file contains the application source code. It's a JavaScript app with three parts we're interested in.

```
'use strict';
var express = require('express'),        ──── 1
    app = express();
app.set('views', 'views');
app.set('view engine', 'pug');             ──── 2
app.get('/', function(req, res) {
    res.render('home', {
  });
});
app.listen(8080);                          ──── 3
module.exports.getApp = app;
```

Figure 4.1. Code from the sample app

1. These lines call the Express module and create a dependency on the Express framework
2. This line sets Pug as the template engine and creates a dependency on Pug
3. This tells the app to listen on port `8080`

The `views/home.pug` file contains a few lines of Pug HTML that display a message on the app's home page.

Feel free to inspect the other two files. `package.json` lists **Express** and **Pug** as dependencies. See bullet points 1 and 2 from the previous list. `package-lock.json` is a lot longer and lists every dependency and sub-dependency within the app.

The current version of `package-lock.json` lists over **90 dependencies** and is a great example of *dependency sprawl*. We often say that we *download the entire internet when we build an app*. This simple app has two dependencies — Express and Pug. However, dependencies have dependencies, which in turn have dependencies. It's dependencies all the way down!

Don't worry if any of that is confusing. All you need to know is that you can use the four files to build an app that displays text on a simple web page.

The folder also has two more files called `sample-compose.yaml` and `sample-Dockerfile`. If you're not using Docker Desktop you'll be able to rename these in later steps to follow the examples.

Test the app

This section is optional and tests the app before containerizing it — there's no point containerizing the app if it doesn't work.

If you choose to complete this section **you'll need to install `Node.js`**. If you install Node.js from the CLI you'll need to quit and restart your shell to pick up the updated PATH variable. If you don't have Node installed, just read this section.

Run the following commands from within the `gsd-book/node-app` directory.

Run an `npm ci` command to install the app dependencies. It downloads all dependencies listed in `package-lock.json` and puts them in a new directory called `node_modules`.

```
$ npm ci
added 97 packages, and audited 98 packages in 756ms
13 packages are looking for funding
  run `npm fund` for details
found 0 vulnerabilities
```

With the packages added, run the following command to start the app. The command will lock your terminal until you kill the app.

```
$ node app.js
```

The app is running. Open a browser and go to `http://localhost:8080/`. You'll see the screen in Figure 4.2.

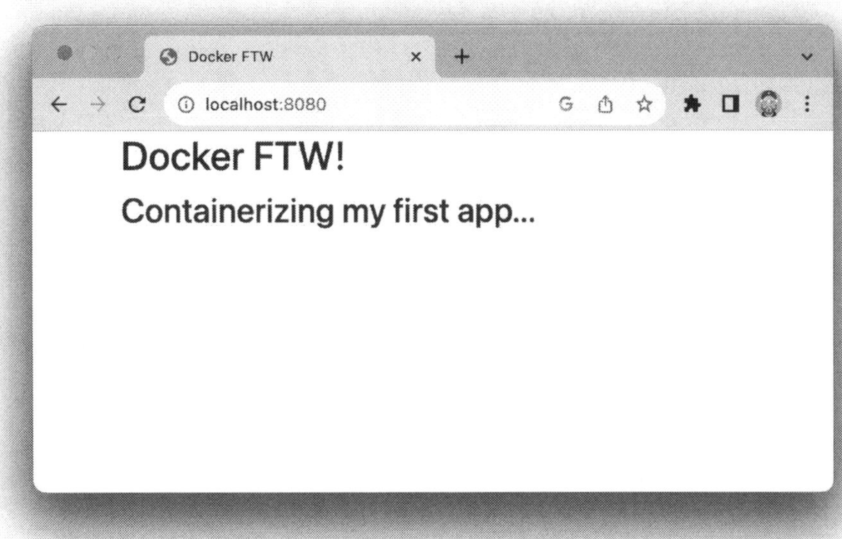

Figure 4.2. App running locally

Success. The app works. Time to containerize it.

Type `Ctrl-c` on the command line to kill the app and free up your terminal.

Containerize the app

The command you're about to run is currently in beta, and all of the following apply:

- The command format and prompts may change
- It only works with Docker Desktop (this may change in the future)

This section walks you through the process of containerizing the app.

Containerization is jargon for packaging the app and all dependencies into a container image. Sometimes we call it *Dockerizing*.

The process can be daunting if you're new to Docker. Even experienced Docker users can find it hard to keep up to date with good practices.

This is where **docker init** comes to the rescue!

`docker init` is a relatively new command. It reads an existing application and produces a high-quality *Dockerfile* that `docker build` can use to containerize the app. It also produces a `.dockerignore` file and a `compose.yaml` file. The `.dockerignore` file helps you keep images small by not copying in unnecessary files, whereas you can use the `compose.yaml` to run and manage the app with *Docker Compose.* More on Docker Compose in Chapter 6.

> **Note:** If you're not using Docker Desktop, you won't be able to run the `docker init` command. Don't worry, though. Just rename the `sample-Dockerfile` to `Dockerfile` and you'll be able to continue with the examples right after the `docker init` command.

Run the following command from within the `gsd-book/node-app` folder. The command should detect the **Node** app. If it doesn't, make sure you're in the right directory and the app files are present.

Complete the prompts as shown. Feel free to accept a more recent version of Node if offered.

```
$ docker init

Welcome to the Docker Init CLI!
Let's get started!

? What application platform does your project use? Node
? What version of Node do you want to use? 20.11.0
? Which package manager do you want to use? npm
? What command do you want to use to start the app? node app.js
? What port does your server listen on? 8080

CREATED: .dockerignore
CREATED: Dockerfile
CREATED: compose.yaml

!Your Docker files are ready!
```

As the output says, your Docker files are ready. If the output tells you to run additional commands, ignore them and only complete the commands listed here in the book.

List the contents of your current directory to see the new `Dockerfile`. Don't worry if you don't see the `.dockerignore` file, it's a hidden file.

```
$ ls -l
-rw-r--r--    1 nigelpoulton  staff    1061 Dockerfile    <<------
-rw-r--r--    1 nigelpoulton  staff     341 app.js
-rw-r--r--    1 nigelpoulton  staff    1681 compose.yaml
drwxr-xr-x   97 nigelpoulton  staff    3104 node_modules
-rw-r--r--    1 nigelpoulton  staff   36757 package-lock.json
-rw-r--r--    1 nigelpoulton  staff     357 package.json
drwxr-xr-x    3 nigelpoulton  staff      96 views
```

At this point, you've got everything you need to containerize the app. However, let's have a quick look at the Dockerfile. If you're not using Docker Desktop and didn't run the `docker init` command, make sure you've renamed the `sample-Dockerfile` to `Dockerfile`.

The following snippet shows the entire Dockerfile with comments removed and line numbers added. I've trimmed lines 5 and 6 to fit the book.

```
1. ARG NODE_VERSION=20.8.0
2.  FROM node:${NODE_VERSION}-alpine
3. ENV NODE_ENV production
4. WORKDIR /usr/src/app
5. RUN --mount=type=bind,source=package.json,target=package.json \
6.      --mount=type=bind,source=package-lock.json,target=pack... \
7.      --mount=type=cache,target=/root/.npm \
8.      npm ci --omit=dev
9. USER node
10. COPY . .
11. EXPOSE 8080
12. CMD node app.js
```

The `docker build` command uses the instructions in the Dockerfile to build the image. It reads the file one line at a time, starting from the top.

Line 1 lists the Node version and is used by line 2 to pull the correct base image. These two lines combine to ensure the `node:20.8.0-alpine` image will be used as the base layer of the new image. Yours may be different if you accepted a newer version of Node when completing the `docker init` prompts.

The **ENV NODE_ENV production** instruction on line 3 tells Node to run in *production mode* for better performance.

Line 4 uses the **WORKDIR** instruction to set the working directory for the rest of the instructions in the file. This means all the following commands and instructions will execute in the image's `/usr/src/app` directory.

The **RUN** instruction is long and spans four lines. The detail isn't super important; you just need to know it implements several best practices for installing dependencies into the image. You should recognise the JSON files and the `npm` command.

The **USER node** instruction on line 9 ensures the app runs as the *node* user and not *root*.

Line 10 copies everything in the same directory as the Dockerfile into the image. However, it ignores any files and directories listed in the `.dockerignore` file.

The **EXPOSE** instruction on line 11 documents the application's network port, and the **CMD** instruction tells Docker which app the container should run.

It's helpful to recognise some of the steps we carried out earlier when we tested the app locally:

- We ran an `npm ci` command to install the dependencies in `package-lock.json`. The Dockerfile mounts `package-lock.json` into the image and runs a similar `npm ci` command.
- We executed the `node app.js` command to start the app. The Dockerfile documents the same command to start the app anytime a container is created.

Now that we understand the Dockerfile, it's time to containerize the app.

Run the following command to build a local image called `node-app`. Notice how the build's output matches the instructions in the Dockerfile. This is because the build steps through the file one line at a time. I've trimmed the output to only show the bits we're interested in.

```
$ docker build -t node-app .
=> [internal] load build definition from Dockerfile        0.0s
=> => transferring dockerfile: 1.10kB                      0.1s
=> [stage-0 1/4] FROM docker.io/library/node:20.8.0-alpine 0.1s
=> CACHED [stage-0 2/4] WORKDIR /usr/src/app               0.0s
=> [stage-0 3/4] RUN --mount=type=bind,source=package.json 0.6s
=> [stage-0 4/4] COPY . .                                  0.1s
=> exporting to image                                      0.6s
<Snip>
View build details: docker-desktop://dashboard/build/...
```

Make sure the image exists.

```
$ docker images
REPOSITORY   TAG      IMAGE ID       CREATED              SIZE
node-app     latest   242fa8fb538b   About a minute ago   267MB
```

Congratulations, you just containerized an app! Time to see if it works.

Test the containerized app

In this section, you'll start a container from the image and connect a browser to see if it works.

Run the following command to start a new container from the image.

```
$ docker run -d --name web -p 8080:8080 node-app
```

Open a browser and go to `http://localhost:8080/`. The app works exactly as it did when we tested it earlier.

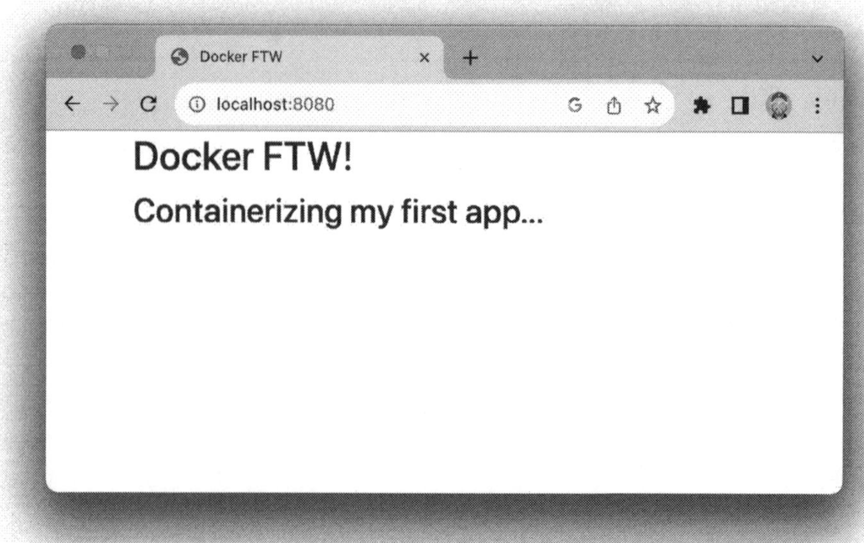

Figure 4.3. App running in a container

Congratulations. You've containerized a Node.js web server and successfully run it as a container.

Now that you've containerized the app, you can push it to Docker Hub and run it on other machines. We'll see this in the next chapter.

Clean-up

Delete the container and the image.

```
$ docker rm web -f
web

$ docker rmi node-app
Untagged: node-app:latest
Deleted: sha256:242fa8fb538bb...
```

Chapter summary

In this chapter, we used `docker init` to containerize a simple Node.js app.

We gave `docker init` some basic information about the app, such as Node version, package manager, network port, and command to start the app. The command produced a `Dockerfile` and `.dockerignore` file implementing good practices. We then used `docker build` to containerize the app by packaging it as an image.

The image contained the app files and all dependencies needed to run the app in a container.

5: Images and registries

This chapter will show you how to build images and work with registries.

I've divided the chapter as follows:

- Working with images
- Working with registries
- Multi-architecture images

Before we start, there are lots of tools to *build* images and lots of registries to *store* them. Fortunately, most of them implement the OCI standards and work well together. For example, Docker and Podman both build *OCI compliant* images and push and pull to *OCI compliant* registries. Similarly, Docker Hub, Artifactory, and GitHub Container Registry are all *OCI-compliant* registries.

We'll focus on `docker build` and Docker Hub to keep things simple.

Working with images

We already know that `docker build` uses a *Dockerfile* to build images. In fact, most other build tools also work with Dockerfiles.

We'll use the following Dockerfile from the *images* folder of the book's GitHub repo. It doesn't implement as many good practices as the one in the previous chapter, but it's a lot easier to explain in a *getting started* book.

```
FROM node:alpine
WORKDIR /usr/src/app
COPY . .
RUN npm ci --omit=dev
USER node
EXPOSE 8080
CMD node app.js
```

The **FROM** instruction pulls the `node:alpine` image and uses it as the new image's base layer.

WORKDIR sets the working directory for the remainder of the commands and instructions.

The **COPY** instruction copies the app files into the image's `/usr/src/app` directory. This includes the JSON files that lists dependencies. There's also a hidden `.dockerignore` file listing files you don't want in the image.

RUN npm ci –omit-dev installs the dependencies into the image.

USER node ensures the app will run as the *node* user and not *root*.

EXPOSE 8080 documents the network port the app listens on.

CMD node app.js tells Docker how to start the app whenever it starts a container from the image.

Figure 5.1 shows the architecture of the final image. It will have four layers and a bunch of metadata that all relates to instructions in the Dockerfile.

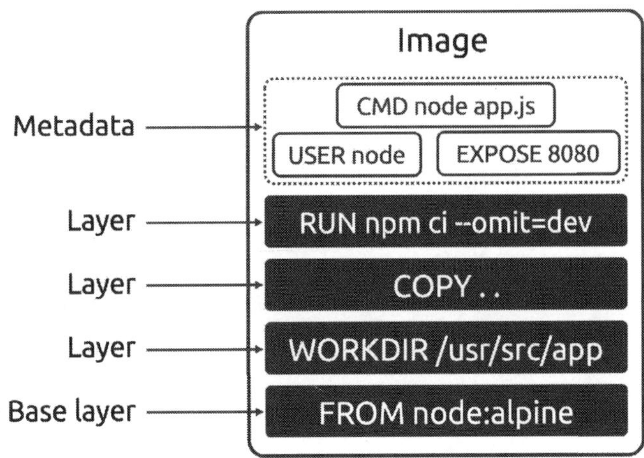

Figure 5.1. Image layers and metadata

Run the following `docker build` command to create a new image called `node-app`. I've trimmed the output so you only see the lines relating to the instructions in the Dockerfile. **Be sure to run it from the 'gsd-book/images' folder.**

```
$ docker build -t node-app .
 => [internal] load build definition from Dockerfile        0.0s
 => => transferring dockerfile: 144B                        0.0s
 => [1/4] FROM docker.io/library/node:alpine...             0.0s
 => CACHED [2/4] WORKDIR /usr/src/app                       0.0s
 => [3/4] COPY . .                                          0.0s
 => [4/4] RUN npm ci --omit=dev                             1.8s
 => exporting to image                                      0.5s
<Snip>
```

Notice the `FROM`, `WORKDIR`, `COPY`, and `RUN` instructions in the output. This is because the build process is stepping through the instructions in the Dockerfile.

You should have a new image called `node-app`.

```
$ docker images
REPOSITORY    TAG       IMAGE ID       CREATED         SIZE
node-app      latest    73b795fd9bc9   5 seconds ago   275MB
```

Notice how Docker has automatically assigned the `latest` tag to the image. This is because Docker is *opinionated* and gives all new images the `latest` tag if you don't specify a different one.

In the next section, you'll push the image to Docker Hub.

Working with registries

Registries are where you securely store container images. Lots of registries exist, and most comply with the *OCI distribution-spec.* We'll use Docker Hub.

You'll need to be signed into a valid Docker account if you want to follow along.

If you don't already have a Docker account, go to `hub.docker.com` and click the **Sign up** button. Accounts are free.

If you already have an account and need to sign in, run the `docker login` command, or click the Docker Desktop whale icon and choose **Sign in/Create Docker ID**.

Once you're signed in, you're ready to go.

The `docker push` command pushes images to Docker Hub and other registries. However, it uses image names to know exactly where to push an image.

Right now, the image you created is called `node-app:latest`. This doesn't give `docker push` enough information, so you'll need to rename it with your Docker username and the name of the repository you want to push it to.

My Docker username is `nigelpoulton`, and I want to push this image to a repository called `gsd-book`. The repository will be created if it doesn't already exist.

The following `docker tag` command will rename the image appropriately. Be sure to replace `nigelpoulton` with your own Docker username. The format of the command is `docker tag <old-name> <new-name>`.

```
$ docker tag node-app nigelpoulton/gsd-book
```

List your local images again.

```
$ docker images
REPOSITORY              TAG      IMAGE ID       CREATED   SIZE
node-app                latest   73b795fd9bc9   33 mins   275MB
nigelpoulton/gsd-book   latest   73b795fd9bc9   33 mins   275MB
```

It might look like there are two images now. However, if you look closely, you'll see it's a single image with two different names — the ID is the same for both.

The image name now has enough info for Docker to push it.

Run the following command to push it to Docker Hub. Be sure to substitute your image name.

```
$ docker push nigelpoulton/gsd-book
Using default tag: latest
Push refers to repository [docker.io/nigelpoulton/gsd-book]
2a2799ae89a2: Pushed
4927cb899c33: Pushed
<Snip>
```

Looking at the first two lines of the output, you'll see that Docker made two assumptions. It *assumed* the `latest` tag, and it also *assumed* you wanted to push it to Docker Hub (docker.io).

You can override both of these on the command line, but not specifying them made the command a lot simpler. For example, if you had to specify both, the command would have been more complex as follows.

```
$ docker push docker.io/nigelpoulton/gsd-book:latest
```

Figure 5.2 shows a fully qualified image name. Docker automatically adds `docker.io` and `latest` if you don't specify anything different.

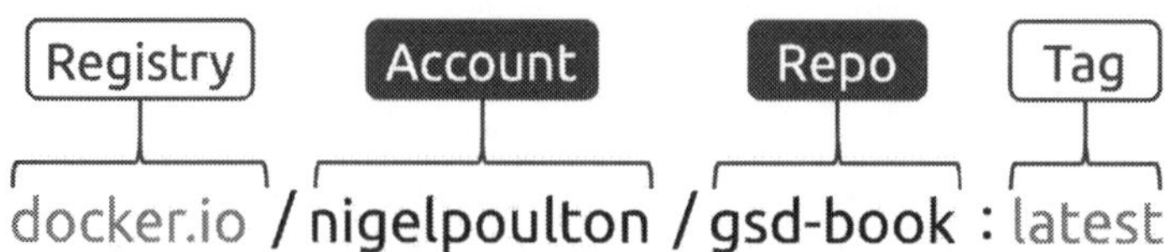

Figure 5.2. Image tag format

Go to Docker Hub and ensure the image is present in the correct repository. Figure 5.3 shows the image on Docker Hub with the relevant items highlighted.

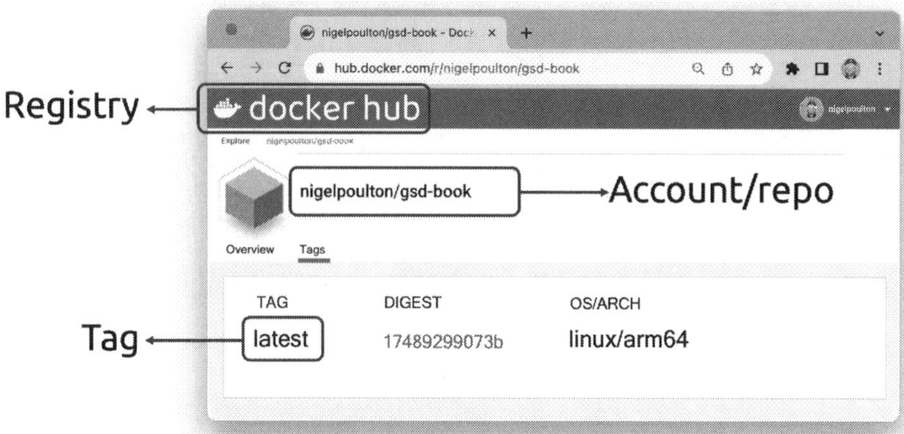

Figure 5.3. Image on Docker Hub

Congratulations, you've built a new image and pushed it to Docker Hub.

However, looking closely at the bottom of Figure 5.3, you'll see the `OS/ARCH` listed as `linux/arm64`. This means the image won't work on Linux hosts running on AMD/x86 architecture.

We'll fix this in the next section.

Multi-architecture images

All container images are built for a specific operating system and CPU architecture. For example:

- Linux on ARM (`linux/arm64`)
- Linux on AMD/x86 (`linux/amd64`)
- Windows on AMD (`windows/amd64`)
- etc.

This creates a common problem where developers might be working on ARM-based Macs, but their production systems are AMD/x86. In this scenario, images built on a developer's Mac won't work in production.

Fortunately, Docker has solutions for this.

Running a `docker build` command with the `--platform` flag allows you to build images for platforms that are different from your Docker host. For example, you can run a `docker build` on a Linux ARM host and have it create images for Linux on AMD/x86. You can even run a single `docker build` command that creates images for multiple platforms.

The following command uses the `--platform` flag to build two images — one for Linux on AMD/x86 and one for Linux on ARM. The `--push` flag pushes the images directly to Docker Hub.

Feel free to run the command. Be sure to substitute your Docker account username.

```
$ docker build \
  --platform=linux/amd64,linux/arm64 \
  -t nigelpoulton/gsd-book:latest \
  --push --no-cache .
```

If you get an error that multi-platform builds are not supported, run the following two commands to create a new builder and set it as default, then run the `docker build` command again, and it should work.

```
$ docker buildx create --driver=docker-container --name=container

$ docker buildx use container
```

Figure 5.4 shows the two images on Docker Hub.

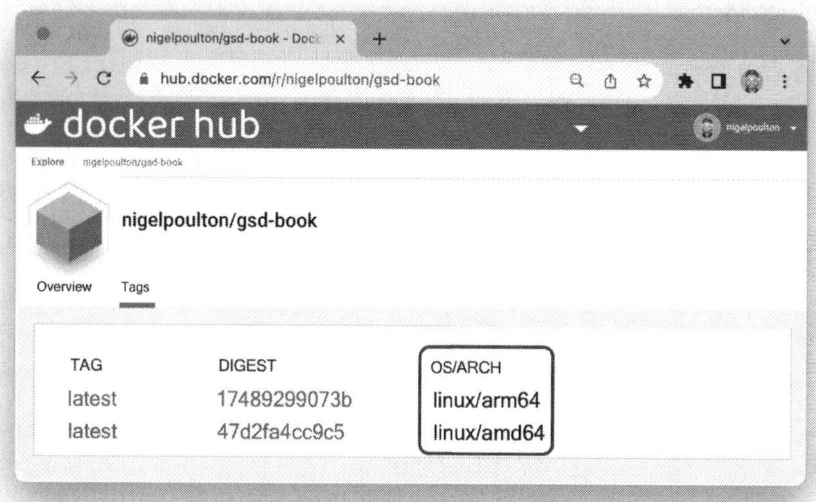

Figure 5.4. Multi-architecture image

Both images are in the same repo with the same name, but Docker is clever enough to pull the correct version for your system. For example, if you run a `docker pull nigelpoulton/gsd-book:latest` on a Linux/AMD system, Docker will pull the AMD version of the image.

Chapter summary

In this chapter, you learned how Docker uses a *Dockerfile* to build new images. The file is just a list of instructions for `docker build` to step through one line at a time, starting from the top.

If you don't specify a tag when working with an image, Docker assumes you mean the `latest` tag. This applies to `docker build`, `docker push`, `docker pull`, `docker run`, and more.

You push images to registries with the `docker push` command. If you don't specify a registry, it assumes you want to push to Docker Hub. The same applies to `docker pull` commands — if you don't specify a registry, it assumes you want to pull from Docker Hub.

`docker build` also lets you build images for lots of different architectures.

Lots of other build tools and registries exist. However, most of them implement the OCI standards and interoperate well.

6: Multi-container apps with Compose

If you've been following along, you've containerized an app, pushed it to a registry, and run it as a container. However, most real-world apps are a lot more complicated and consist of many different containers working together. We call these *multi-container apps* or *microservices apps*.

In this chapter, you'll use *Docker Compose* to deploy and manage a simple multi-container app. The goal is for you to understand the fundamentals of multi-container apps and gain some hands-on experience with Compose.

I've divided the chapter into the following sections:

- Overview of the app
- The Compose file
- Deploy the app
- Manage the app

Overview of the app

The application we're about to deploy has two containers (microservices):

- web
- store

The **web** container runs a Python flask app that displays a simple web page with a picture, some text, and a counter. The app counts the number of page refreshes and stores the value in a Redis database in the **store** container. If you refresh the page 10 times, the counter in the database will increment each time, and the web page will display the current counter value.

Figure 6.1 shows an overview of the app. The page has been refreshed four times in the image.

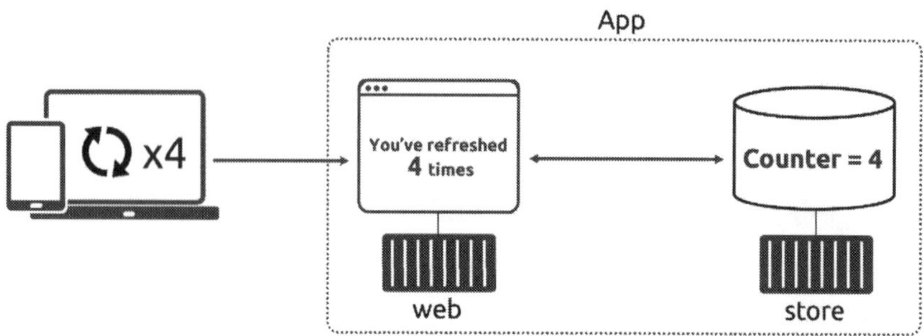

Figure 6.1. The app.

Let's see how to define this app in a configuration file that Docker can use to deploy and manage it.

The Compose file

Compose is a popular tool for deploying and managing multi-container apps. You define the app in a *Compose file* and then use the `docker compose` command to deploy and manage it.

Figure 6.2 shows the *Compose file* we'll be using. It's called `compose.yaml`, and you can find it in the `compose-app` folder of the book's GitHub repo. As shown in the diagram, it defines two containers and a network.

Compose refers to containers as *services*; this file defines one called **web** and another called **store**. It also defines a network called **internal**.

```
1.  networks:
2.    internal:
3.  services:
4.    web:
5.      build: .
6.      command: python app.py
7.      ports:
8.        - target: 8080
9.          published: 5555
10.     networks:
11.       - internal
12.   store:
13.     image: "redis:alpine"
14.     networks:
15.       - internal
```

web

store

Figure 6.2. The Compose file.

Let's quickly step through it.

The first two lines define a network called *internal*. Docker Compose will read these lines and create a container network called *internal*.

Line 3 defines a new block called *services*. Both of the containers are defined under this block.

Lines 4-11 define the *web* service (container). Line 5 tells Docker to build the image for this container from the Dockerfile in the same directory. Line 6 is the command the container should run to start the app. Lines 7-9 map port `8080` inside the container to port `5555` on the Docker host. Finally, lines 10-11 attach the container to the *internal* network.

Lines 12-15 define another service (container) called *store*. Line 13 tells Docker to pull the `redis:alpine` image for this container, and lines 14 and 15 attach it to the same *internal* network.

Figure 6.3 shows the overall configuration. It shows the **web** and **store** containers both connected to the **internal** network. The **web** container maps port `8080` inside the container to `5555` on the host. The **web** container also connects to the **store** container on port `6379`.

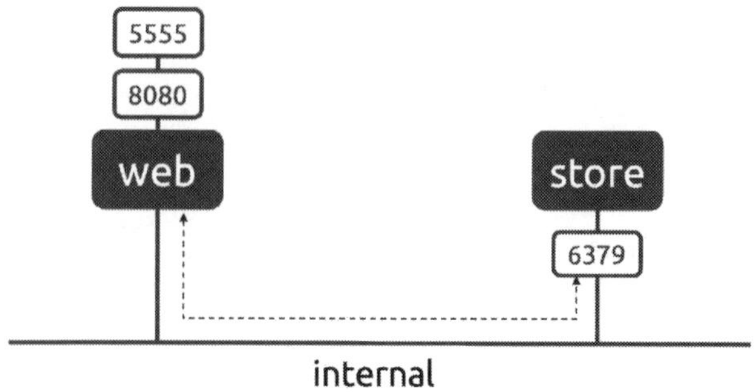

Figure 6.3

The connection from the **web** container to the **store** container on port `6379` isn't defined in the Compose file. However, `6379` is the default port Redis listens on, and the following snippet shows where it's defined in the `app.py` file.

```
import time
import redis
from flask import Flask, render_template

app = Flask(__name__)
cache = redis.Redis(host='store', port=6379)    <<------
<snip>
```

One last thing about the Compose file before we deploy the app. Line 5 tells Docker to *build* the image for the **web** container. This means Docker will automatically build the image when you deploy the app. It will use the Dockerfile in the same directory.

```
1. networks:
2.   internal:
3. services:
4.   web:
5.     build: .                <<------ This line
6.     command: python app.py
7.     <Snip>
```

Deploy the app

You'll need a copy of the book's GitHub repo to follow along. If you haven't already got it, run the following command.

```
$ git clone https://github.com/nigelpoulton/gsd-book.git
```

Be sure to run the following commands from within the `gsd-book/compose-app` folder. You should have all of these files and folders in your current directory.

```
$ ls -l
-rw-r--r--@ 1 nigelpoulton  staff  528  Dockerfile
-rw-r--r--@ 1 nigelpoulton  staff  594  app.py
-rw-r--r--@ 1 nigelpoulton  staff  283  compose.yaml
-rw-r--r--@ 1 nigelpoulton  staff   18  requirements.txt
drwxr-xr-x  5 nigelpoulton  staff  160  static
drwxr-xr-x  4 nigelpoulton  staff  128  templates
```

Run the following `docker compose` command to bring up the app. The command reads the `compose.yaml` file in your current directory and deploys everything defined in it.

```
$ docker compose up --detach
[+] store Pulling...
[+] Building...
<Snip>
[+] Running 3/3
 - Network compose-app_internal     Created              0.0s
 - Container compose-app-store-1    Started              0.1s
 - Container compose-app-web-1      Started              0.0s
```

If you look at the output, you'll notice Docker *pulling* the image for the **store** container and then *building* the image for the **web** container. After that, it creates the **internal** network and starts the two containers. As part of the operation, it connects both containers to the **internal** network and does all of the port mappings.

Run a `docker compose ps` command to list the containers in the app. I've trimmed the output to fit the book, but it shows both containers and is similar to the output of a `docker ps` command.

```
$ docker compose ps
NAME                 SERVICE  IMAGE            PORTS
compose-app-store-1  store    redis:alpine     6379/tcp
compose-app-web-1    web      compose-app-web  0.0.0.0:5555->8080
```

Both containers are up, and the multi-container app is running!

Notice how Docker has prefixed container names with the name of the working directory ("compose-app"). This is because Compose uses the name of your current directory as the *project name* to help you distinguish between multiple Compose projects.

Run a `docker network ls` to ensure the **internal** network was created.

```
$ docker network ls
NETWORK ID     NAME                  DRIVER   SCOPE
63e63ec84ae1   bridge                bridge   local
0c55ba331291   compose-app_internal  bridge   local  <<----
9b4509c1b8a4   host                  host     local
86afd80b6872   none                  null     local
```

Even the network name is prefixed with the project name.

If you're following along with Docker Desktop, connect a browser to `http://localhost:5555/` and click refresh a few times. The counter will increment with each refresh.

If you're following along on Multipass, connect a browser to port `5555` on your Multipass VM's **192** IP address. You can get this by running a `multipass list` from outside the VM. As an example, if your Multipass VM's IP address is `192.168.64.58`, point your browser to `http://192.168.64.58:5555`.

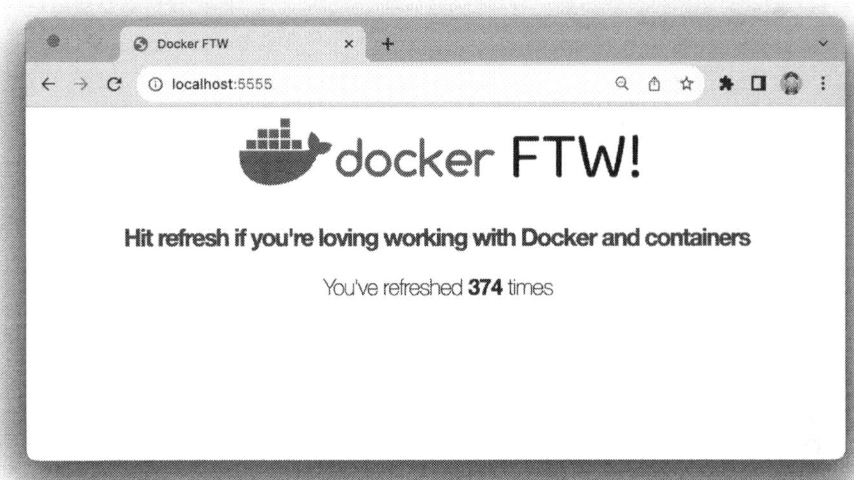

Congratulations. You've successfully deployed a multi-container app with a web front end and a Redis data store back end.

Manage the app

The `docker compose` command lets you perform lifecycle operations such as stopping, starting, restarting, and deleting the app.

Performing *updates* is typically done by updating the `compose.yaml` file and running another `docker compose up`.

We'll complete the following steps:

- Stop the app
- Restart the app
- Update the app
- Delete the app

Stop the app

Run a `docker compose ls` to check the current status of the app.

```
$ docker compose ls
NAME          STATUS       CONFIG FILES
compose-app   running(2)   .../gsd-book/compose-app/compose.yaml
```

The `STATUS` column shows the app is *running* with *2* containers.

Stop it with the following command. As with all `docker compose` commands, it reads the `compose.yaml` file in the current directory.

```
$ docker compose stop
[+] Stopping 2/2
 - Container compose-app-store-1   Stopped            0.1s
 - Container compose-app-web-1     Stopped            0.2s
```

The app is down, so refreshing your browser will timeout.

Restart the app

Run the following command to restart the app.

```
$ docker compose restart
[+] Restarting 2/2
 - Container compose-app-store-1   Started            0.3s
 - Container compose-app-web-1     Started            0.3s
```

Refresh your browser and confirm the app is back up and running. Notice how the counter wasn't reset. This is because the containers were only *stopped,* and stopped containers don't lose data.

Update the app

Compose apps are *declarative*. This means you should do updates by making changes to the `compose.yaml` file and then re-deploying the app from the updated file.

Let's do it.

The app has two features — a web server and a data store. As this is a *microservices* app, each feature is deployed as its own small application inside its own container. This means we can update the web server without impacting the data store.

Edit the `compose.yaml` file and delete the **build** instruction under the **web** service. Replace it with an **image** instruction telling it to use the `nigelpoulton/gsd-book:banner` image. The following snippet shows which line to delete and which line to add.

```
networks:
  internal:
services:
  web:
    build: .                               <<--- Delete this line
    image: nigelpoulton/gsd-book:banner    <<--- Add this line
    command: python app.py
    <Snip>
```

Be sure to get the indentation right and save your changes.

Once you've saved your changes, run the following command to update the app. As you've only changed the **web** service, Docker will only make changes to that, and will leave the **store** service alone. The `--pull always` flag forces Docker to pull the latest images for both services (containers) will be.

```
$ docker compose up --pull always --detach
[+] Running 2/2
 - store Pulled                                          1.6s
 - web Pulled                                            1.5s
[+] Building 0.0s (0/0)
[+] Running 2/2
 - Container compose-app-store-1      Running            0.0s
 - Container compose-app-web-1        Started            0.2s
```

The output shows Docker pulling both images but only restarting the **web** container.

Refresh your browser to see the change.

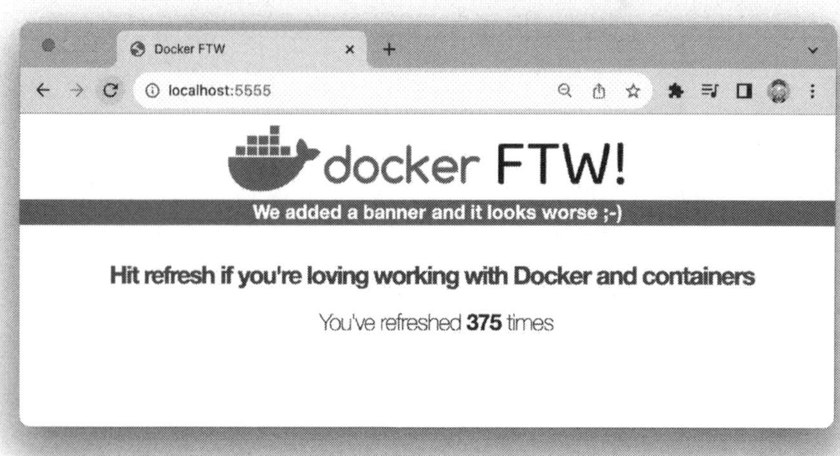

The updated web container has a banner below the image.

Notice that the counter didn't reset. This is because we only made changes to the **web** service. If this had been a *monolithic app*, the change would have required the entire application to be taken offline and restarted.

Congratulations. You've defined, deployed, managed, and updated a multi-container microservices app!

Delete the app

Run the following command to delete the app. The command will delete both containers and the network. Specifying the `--rmi all` flag ensures all images relating to the app also get deleted.

```
$ docker compose down --rmi all
[+] Running 6/6
 - Container compose-app-store-1       Removed       0.2s
 - Container compose-app-web-1         Removed       0.2s
 - Image redis:alpine                  Removed       0.1s
 - Image nigelpoulton/gsd-book:banner  Removed       0.1s
 - Image compose-app-web:latest        Removed       0.1s
 - Network compose-app_internal        Removed       0.1s
```

The output shows the containers, images, and network being deleted.

Chapter summary

In this chapter, you learned about Docker Compose and how to use it to deploy and manage multi-container apps.

You define multi-container apps in *Compose* files and use the `docker compose up` command to deploy the app from the file. Docker reads the file and deploys everything in it.

The `docker compose` command lets you easily perform lifecycle operations such as stopping, restarting, and deleting the app.

You should update applications declaratively by modifying the Compose file and re-deploying the app with another `docker compose up`.

7: Docker and WebAssembly

WebAssembly is driving the next wave of cloud computing, and Docker is evolving to take advantage.

In this chapter, you'll write a simple WebAssembly app and use Docker to containerize and run it in a container. The goal is to introduce you to WebAssembly and show you how easy it is to work with Docker and WebAssembly together.

The terms *WebAssembly* and *Wasm* mean the same thing and we'll use the term Wasm.

I've divided the chapter as follows:

- Pre-reqs
- Intro to Wasm
- Write a Wasm app
- Containerize a Wasm app
- Deploy a Wasm app

Pre-reqs

You'll need all of the following if you plan on following along:

- Docker Desktop **4.27**+ with Wasm enabled
- Rust 1.72+ with the Wasm target installed
- Spin 2.4+

At the time of writing, support for Wasm is a beta feature in Docker Desktop and doesn't work with Multipass Docker VMs. This may change in the future. It also means there's a higher risk of bugs. The examples in this chapter have been tested on Docker Desktop 4.27.1 and 4.28.0.

Configure Docker Desktop for Wasm

You'll need Docker Desktop 4.27.1 or later to follow along.

At the time of writing, support for Wasm in Docker Desktop is experimental, and you need to enable it manually. This will change in the future.

Open the Docker Desktop UI, click the Settings icon at the top right, click the **Features in development** tab, and enable the following:

- Enable Wasm

If the option is greyed out (unavailable) you'll have to enable `Use containerd for pulling and storing images` on the `General` tab first.

Click **Apply & restart**. The settings are shown in Figure 7.1.

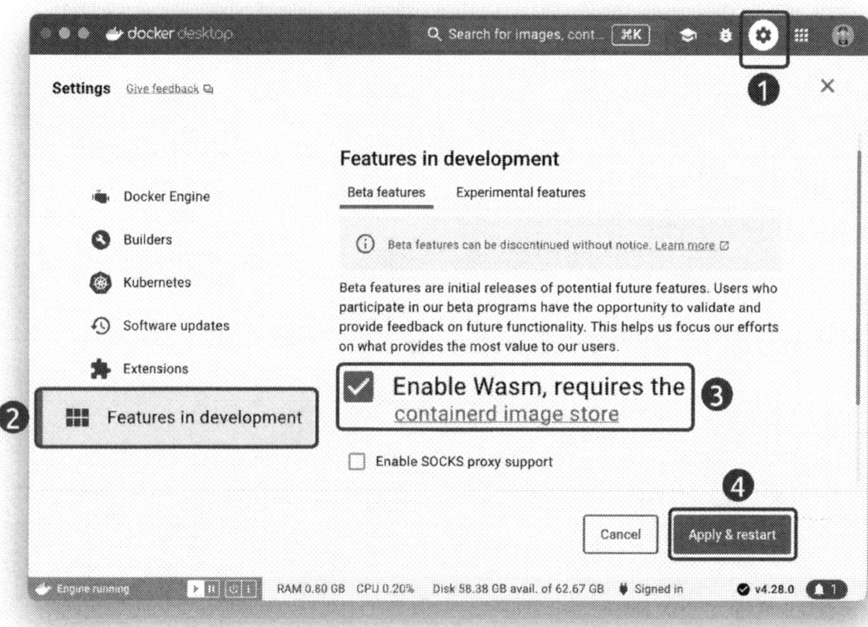

Figure 7.1. Docker Desktop Wasm settings

Install Rust and configure for Wasm

Search the web for *how to install Rust* and follow the instructions for your platform.

Once you've installed Rust, run the following command to install the `wasm32-wasi` target. This is what allows Rust to compile to Wasm.

```
$ rustup target add wasm32-wasi
info: downloading component 'rust-std' for 'wasm32-wasi'
info: installing component 'rust-std' for 'wasm32-wasi'
```

Install Spin

Search the web for *how to install Fermyon spin* and follow the instructions for your system.

Run the following command to ensure it's installed correctly.

```
$ spin --version
spin 2.4.2 (340378e 2024-04-03)
```

You're now ready to follow along.

Intro to Wasm

At a very high level, Wasm is a new type of application that is smaller, faster, and more portable than traditional containers. However, traditional containers can do a lot more than Wasm apps. For example, Wasm apps are currently great for serverless functions, plugins, and edge devices, but not so good for complex networking or heavy I/O.

That was very high level, and Wasm is evolving fast.

Digging a little deeper…

As we're about to see, Wasm is a new virtual machine architecture that programming languages compile to. So, instead of compiling apps for platforms such as *Linux on ARM* or *Linux on AMD*, we can compile them to *Wasm*. These Wasm apps will then run on any system with a *Wasm runtime*. Fortunately, Docker Desktop already ships with several *Wasm runtimes.*

The take-home point is this... Docker Desktop can package and run traditional Linux containers **and** Wasm containers.

Let's see it in action.

Write a Wasm app

We'll use **spin** to create a simple web server that we'll compile as a Wasm app.

Spin is a Wasm framework that makes building and working with Wasm apps easy.

Run the following command to create the app and call it *hello-world*. Respond to the prompts as shown in the example.

```
$ spin new hello-world -t http-rust
Description: Wasm app
HTTP path: /hello
```

The command creates a new directory called **hello-world**. Change into this directory and inspect the files it created. If your system doesn't have the `tree` command, run an `ls -l` for similar results.

```
$ cd hello-world

$ tree
.
├── Cargo.toml
├── spin.toml
└── src
    └── lib.rs
```

We're only interested in two files — `lib.rs` and `spin.toml`.

Edit the `src/lib.rs` file and change the text inside the double quotes, as shown in the following snippet. The goal is to configure the app to display *Docker loves Wasm.*

```
use spin_sdk::http::{IntoResponse, Request};
<Snip>
    Ok(http::Response::builder()
        .status(200)
        .header("content-type", "text/plain")
        .body("Docker loves Wasm")?)   <<---- Change
}
```

Once you've saved your changes, run a `spin build` command to compile the app as a Wasm binary.

```
$ spin build
Building component with `cargo build --target wasm32-wasi --release`
<Snip>
Finished building all Spin components
```

If you look at the first line of the output, you'll see it's running a more complex `cargo build` command to compile the app as a Wasm binary.

Run another `tree` command to see the Wasm binary. *Wasm binary* is jargon for *Wasm app*.

```
$ tree
<Snip>
└── target
    └── wasm32-wasi
        └── release
            └── hello_world.wasm
```

The output is much longer this time, and the example in the book is heavily trimmed to only show the Wasm app. This app (`hello_world.wasm`) will run on any system with the **spin** Wasm runtime, including Docker Desktop.

Congratulations. You just built a simple web server and compiled it into a Wasm app!

Containerize a Wasm app

Docker Desktop supports containerizing Wasm apps. This means we can use regular Docker tools to push and pull Wasm apps to OCI registries and run Wasm apps inside containers.

As always, we need a Dockerfile that tells Docker how to package the app as an image. Create a new file called **Dockerfile** in your current directory and populate it with the following three lines. The file is available in the **wasm** folder of the book's GitHub repo[3] if you prefer to copy and paste the contents.

```
FROM scratch
COPY /target/wasm32-wasi/release/hello_world.wasm .
COPY spin.toml .
```

This Dockerfile uses a special empty base image called *scratch*. We use this because Wasm doesn't need a Linux OS like a traditional container.

The two **COPY** instructions copy the Wasm app and the `spin.toml` file into the image.

That's all that's needed to containerize this Wasm app.

[3]https://github.com/nigelpoulton/gsd-book/blob/main/wasm/Dockerfile

The `spin.toml` file expects the Wasm app to be in the `target/wasm32-wasi/release/` directory. However, the second `COPY` instruction in the Dockerfile places it in the root folder. This means we'll need to update the `spin.toml` file before it gets put into the image.

Edit the `spin.toml` file and remove the leading path for the **source** line as shown.

```
<Snip>
[component.hello-world]
source = "hello_world.wasm"        <<------ Change to this
<Snip>
```

Save your changes.

The Wasm app is ready to be containerized.

Run the following command. The `--platform wasi/wasm` flag sets the image as a Wasm image. Be sure to tag the image with your Docker username instead of mine.

```
$ docker build \
  --platform wasi/wasm \
  --provenance=false \
  -t nigelpoulton/gsd-book:wasm .
```

Some older versions of Docker have an older builder and will fail. If this happens, try running the same command, but change the first line to `docker buildx build \`.

Run a `docker images` command to list the new image. See how it looks like a regular image, just smaller.

```
$ docker images
REPOSITORY              TAG    IMAGE ID       CREATED       SIZE
nigelpoulton/gsd-book   wasm   1fb247c79452   8 secs ago    556kB
```

You can `push` and `pull` the image to Docker Hub and other OCI registries as normal.

The following command pushes the image to one of my repos in Docker Hub. Be sure to tag the image with your own Docker username.

```
$ docker push nigelpoulton/gsd-book:wasm
```

If you look on Docker Hub, you can see Docker Hub has recognised it as a **wasi/wasm** image.

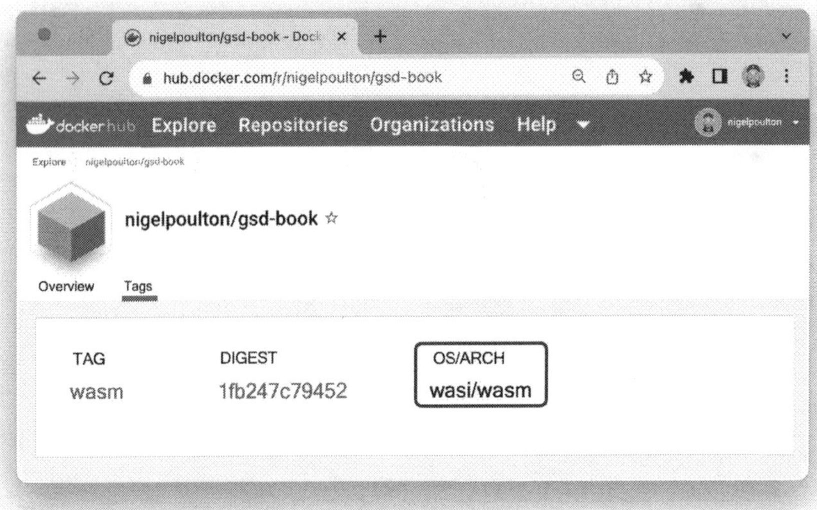

Figure 7.2. Wasm image on Docker Hub

Deploy a Wasm app

Now the Wasm app is packaged as an OCI image, you can run it in a container with the `docker run` command.

The following command runs it in a new container called `wasm-ctr` and maps it to port `5556` on the Docker host. The `--runtime` flag makes sure Docker uses the **spin** Wasm runtime to execute it. Versions of Docker Desktop older than 4.24 may not have the **spin** runtime and will fail.

```
$ docker run -d --name wasm-ctr \
  --runtime=io.containerd.spin.v1 \
  --platform=wasi/wasm \
  -p 5556:80 \
  nigelpoulton/gsd-book:wasm /
```

You can check it's running with a regular `docker ps` command.

Connect a browser to `http://localhost:5556/hello` to see the app.

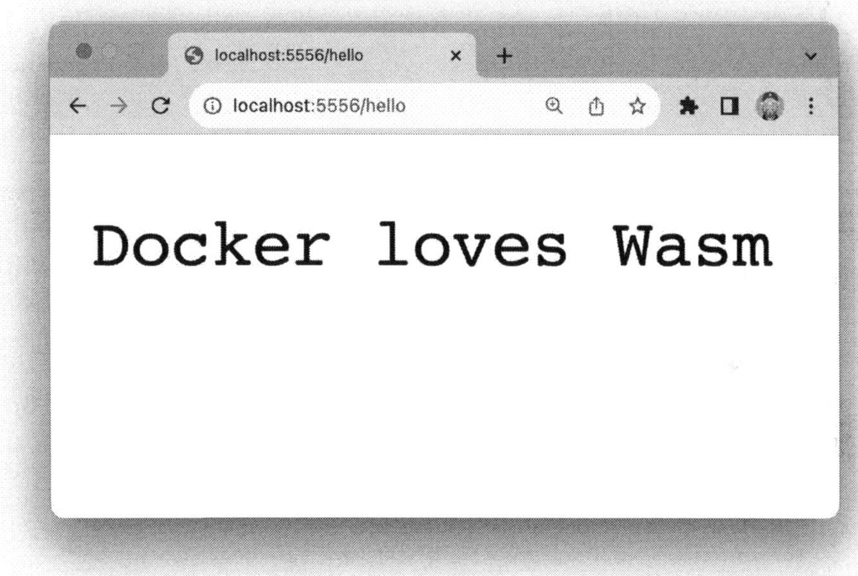

Figure 7.3. Running Wasm app

Congratulations, the app is running inside a Docker container. We sometimes call these *Wasm containers* to distinguish them from traditional *Linux containers*.

Clean up

Run the following commands to delete the container and the local image.

```
$ docker rm wasm-ctr -f
wasm-ctr

$ docker rmi nigelpoulton/gsd-book:wasm
Untagged: nigelpoulton/gsd-book:wasm
Deleted: sha256:1fb247c79452...
```

You'll still have a copy of the image on Docker Hub. Feel free to delete that as well.

Chapter summary

In this chapter, you containerized a Wasm app and ran it in a container.

Wasm is a new technology driving the next wave of cloud computing. Wasm apps are smaller, faster, more secure, and more portable than traditional containers. However, they're not as flexible. For example, at the time of writing, Wasm apps aren't great for apps with heavy I/O requirements or complex networking. This will change quickly as the Wasm ecosystem is evolving fast.

Fortunately, Docker has already evolved to work with Wasm, and Docker Desktop ships with lots of popular Wasm runtimes. This enables us to use industry-standard tools, such as `docker build` and `docker run`, to containerize and run Wasm apps. You can even push them to OCI registries such as Docker Hub.

8: What next

Congratulations on finishing the book. I hope you enjoyed it.

Where you go next depends entirely on you. However, if you followed along and completed all the examples, you've taken a huge step forward and gained some valuable skills.

- If you're a developer, you're ready to start containerizing apps
- If you're DevOps, or any of the many other xOps, you're ready to start using Docker in your work projects
- If you're in technical marketing or sales, you're ready to start speaking publicly about Docker and containers
- If you're an architect or in management, you know enough to start making informed decisions

Here are a few ideas of what to do next…

Hands-on

Get as much hands-on as possible, and Docker Desktop is a great place to start.

Books

If you like books and want to continue your Docker journey, check out my **Docker Deep Dive** book. It follows on from here and goes into a lot more detail.

If you liked this book and want a similar introduction to Kubernetes, check out my **Quick Start Kubernetes** book.

Both are available from all good book resellers.

Videos

If you like video courses, I've got lots on pluralsight.com. They're a lot of fun and apparently *"laugh out loud funny"* — not my words.

Events

I highly recommend you attend local Docker and cloud-native (CNCF) meet-ups. And if you can afford it, you should attend DockerCon!

Events like these are full of great content and amazing people. If you see me hanging around at an event, please come and say hi!

Let's connect

Finally, thanks again for reading my book. Feel free to connect with me on any of the usual platforms to discuss Docker and other cool technologies.

- linkedin.com/in/nigelpoulton
- @nigelpoulton@hachyderm.io
- @nigelpoulton
- @nigelpoulton.bsky.social
- gsd@nigelpoulton.com

Appendix A: Lab code

This appendix contains all the command-line demos in one convenient place.

Pre-reqs

You'll need all of the following if you plan on completing *all* demos:

- A clone of the book's GitHub repo
- Docker Desktop 4.27.1 or higher with Wasm support enabled
- Rust 1.72+ with the `wasm32-wasi` target installed
- Spin 2.4+
- A Docker account

Search the internet for instructions on how to install each requirement.

Once installed, run the following commands to clone the book's GitHub repo and install the `wasm32-wasi` Rust target.

```
$ git clone https://github.com/nigelpoulton/gsd-book.git
Cloning into 'gsd-book'...
remote: Enumerating objects: 53, done.
remote: Counting objects: 100% (53/53), done.
remote: Compressing objects: 100% (36/36), done.
remote: Total 53 (delta 18), reused 43 (delta 10), pack-reused 0
Receiving objects: 100% (53/53), 52.97 KiB | 763.00 KiB/s, done.
Resolving deltas: 100% (18/18), done.

$ rustup target add wasm32-wasi
info: downloading component 'rust-std' for 'wasm32-wasi'
info: installing component 'rust-std' for 'wasm32-wasi'
 18.1 MiB /  18.1 MiB (100 %)  17.3 MiB/s in  1s ETA:  0s
```

With all of these installed, you're ready to complete the demos.

Chapter 3: Running your first container

Check for existing images and containers on your system.

```
$ docker images
REPOSITORY   TAG       IMAGE ID   CREATED   SIZE

$ docker ps
CONTAINER ID   IMAGE     COMMAND    STATUS     PORTS     NAMES
```

Create a new container called `test`.

```
$ docker run -d --name test -p 5555:8080 nigelpoulton/gsd-book

Unable to find image 'nigelpoulton/gsd-book:latest' locally
latest: Pulling from nigelpoulton/gsd-book
ee605d576664: Download complete
4f4fb700ef54: Download complete
53062d7cc4ed: Download complete
bdb2de7ba06c: Download complete
56b352bc4d6a: Download complete
Digest: sha256:262ad15072366133dc...7290cef95634f237556056
Status: Downloaded newer image for nigelpoulton/gsd-book:latest
f879f4b0571022dad8197be14db222ef75b5280f4b02a804632d30b8381bb88d
```

Check the container is running.

```
$ docker ps
CTR ID    IMAGE                   ...  PORTS                  NAMES
f89..710  nigelpoulton/gsd-book   ...  0.0.0.0:5555->8080     test
```

Test it works by opening a browser to `http://localhost:5555/`.

Stop the container. It may take 10 seconds to gracefully stop.

```
$ docker stop test
```

Restart it.

```
$ docker start test
```

Delete it.

```
$ docker rm test -f
```

Chapter 4: Containerizing an application

Run these commands from within the **gsd-book/node-app** folder of the book's GitHub repo.

We're only showing the container-related demos from this chapter. We're not replicating the local Node.js testing.

List the application files.

```
$ ls -l
-rw-r--r--  1 nigelpoulton  staff    341  app.js
-rw-r--r--  1 nigelpoulton  staff  36757  package-lock.json
-rw-r--r--  1 nigelpoulton  staff    357  package.json
drwxr-xr-x  3 nigelpoulton  staff     96  views
```

Scaffold a new Dockerfile to containerize the app. Complete the prompts as shown and feel free to accept a newer version of Node if offered.

```
$ docker init

Welcome to the Docker Init CLI!
Let's get started!

? What application platform does your project use?  Node
? What version of Node do you want to use?  20.8.0
? Which package manager do you want to use?  npm
? What command do you want to use to start the app?  node app.js
? What port does your server listen on?  8080

CREATED: .dockerignore
CREATED: Dockerfile
CREATED: compose.yaml

!Your Docker files are ready!
```

Containerize the app.

```
$ docker build -t node-app .
=> [internal] load build definition from Dockerfile         0.0s
=> => transferring dockerfile: 1.10kB                        0.1s
=> [stage-0 1/4] FROM docker.io/library/node:20.8.0-alpine  0.1s
=> CACHED [stage-0 2/4] WORKDIR /usr/src/app                0.0s
=> [stage-0 3/4] RUN --mount=type=bind,source=package.json  0.6s
=> [stage-0 4/4] COPY . .                                   0.1s
=> exporting to image                                       0.6s
<Snip>
View build details: docker-desktop://dashboard/build/...
```

Check the image was created.

```
$ docker images
REPOSITORY   TAG      IMAGE ID       CREATED               SIZE
node-app     latest   242fa8fb538b   About a minute ago   267MB
```

Run it as a container.

```
$ docker run -d --name web -p 8080:8080 node-app
```

Test the app with a browser.

Open a browser and go to `http://localhost:8080/`.

Delete the container and the image.

```
$ docker rm web -f
web

$ docker rmi node-app
Untagged: node-app:latest
Deleted: sha256:242fa8fb538bb...
```

Chapter 5: Images and Registries

Run the following commands from within the **images** folder of the book's GitHub repo.

Check the Dockerfile.

```
$ cat Dockerfile

FROM node:alpine
WORKDIR /usr/src/app
COPY . .
RUN npm ci --omit=dev
USER node
EXPOSE 8080
CMD node app.js
```

Build the image and call it **node-app**.

```
$ docker build -t node-app .
 => [internal] load build definition from Dockerfile       0.0s
 => => transferring dockerfile: 144B                       0.0s
 => [1/4] FROM docker.io/library/node:alpine...            0.0s
 => CACHED [2/4] WORKDIR /usr/src/app                      0.0s
 => [3/4] COPY . .                                         0.0s
 => [4/4] RUN npm ci --omit=dev                            1.8s
 => exporting to image                                     0.5s
<Snip>
```

Check the image created.

```
$ docker images
REPOSITORY   TAG      IMAGE ID       CREATED         SIZE
node-app     latest   73b795fd9bc9   5 seconds ago   275MB
```

Rename the image so you can push it to one of **your** repositories on Docker Hub. Be sure to use your Docker Hub username instead of mine.

```
$ docker tag node-app nigelpoulton/gsd-book
```

Push the image to Docker Hub. Be sure to substitute your repo name.

```
$ docker push nigelpoulton/gsd-book
Using default tag: latest
Push refers to repository [docker.io/nigelpoulton/gsd-book]
2a2799ae89a2: Pushed
4927cb899c33: Pushed
<Snip>
```

Go to Docker Hub and check it uploaded correctly.

Run the following command to build and automatically **push** a `linux/arm64` and a `linux/amd64` image to Docker Hub.

```
$ docker build \
  --platform=linux/amd64,linux/arm64 \
  -t nigelpoulton/gsd-book:latest \
  --push --no-cache .
```

Go to Docker Hub and verify they pushed correctly.

Chapter 6: Multi-container apps

Run the following commands from within the **gsd-book/compose-app** folder of the book's GitHub repo.

List the files in your current directory.

```
$ ls -l
-rw-r--r--@ 1 nigelpoulton  staff  528  Dockerfile
-rw-r--r--@ 1 nigelpoulton  staff  594  app.py
-rw-r--r--@ 1 nigelpoulton  staff  283  compose.yaml
-rw-r--r--@ 1 nigelpoulton  staff   18  requirements.txt
drwxr-xr-x  5 nigelpoulton  staff  160  static
drwxr-xr-x  4 nigelpoulton  staff  128  templates
```

Start the Compose app.

```
$ docker compose up --detach
[+] store Pulling...
[+] Building...
<Snip>
[+] Running 3/3
 - Network compose-app_internal     Created              0.0s
 - Container compose-app-store-1    Started              0.1s
 - Container compose-app-web-1      Started              0.0s
```

List the containers that are part of the app.

```
$ docker compose ps
NAME                 SERVICE   IMAGE             PORTS
compose-app-store-1  store     redis:alpine      6379/tcp
compose-app-web-1    web       compose-app-web   0.0.0.0:5555->8080
```

Check the **internal** network was created. It will show as **compose-app_internal**.

```
$ docker network ls
NETWORK ID     NAME                   DRIVER   SCOPE
63e63ec84ae1   bridge                 bridge   local
0c55ba331291   compose-app_internal   bridge   local   <<----
9b4509c1b8a4   host                   host     local
86afd80b6872   none                   null     local
```

Check the current state of the app.

```
$ docker compose ls
NAME          STATUS       CONFIG FILES
compose-app   running(2)   .../gsd-book/compose-app/compose.yaml
```

Connect a browser to `http://localhost:5555/` and click refresh a few times. The counter will increment with each refresh.

Stop the app.

```
$ docker compose stop
[+] Stopping 2/2
 - Container compose-app-store-1   Stopped            0.1s
 - Container compose-app-web-1     Stopped            0.2s
```

Restart it.

```
$ docker compose restart
[+] Restarting 2/2
 - Container compose-app-store-1   Started              0.3s
 - Container compose-app-web-1     Started              0.3s
```

Edit the `compose.yaml` file and make the following changes.

```
networks:
  internal:
services:
  web:
    build: .                              <<--- Delete this line
    image: nigelpoulton/gsd-book:banner  <<--- Add this line
    command: python app.py
    <Snip>
```

Save your changes and redeploy the app.

```
$ docker compose up --pull always --detach
[+] Running 2/2
 - store Pulled                                         1.6s
 - web Pulled                                           1.5s
[+] Building 0.0s (0/0)
[+] Running 2/2
 - Container compose-app-store-1     Running            0.0s
 - Container compose-app-web-1       Started            0.2s
```

Connect a browser to `http://localhost:5555/` to see the change.

Delete the app and all app-related images.

```
$ docker compose down --rmi all
[+] Running 6/6
 - Container compose-app-store-1         Removed        0.2s
 - Container compose-app-web-1           Removed        0.2s
 - Image redis:alpine                    Removed        0.1s
 - Image nigelpoulton/gsd-book:banner    Removed        0.1s
 - Image compose-app-web:latest          Removed        0.1s
 - Network compose-app_internal          Removed        0.1s
```

Chapter 7: Docker and WebAssembly

You'll need Docker Desktop 4.27.1 or later with Wasm support enabled. You'll also need spin 2.4 or later.

Run these commands from within a new empty folder.

Use **spin** to create a new Rust web app.

```
$ spin new hello-world -t http-rust
Description: Wasm app
HTTP path: /hello
```

Edit the `src/lib.rs` file and change the text inside the double quotes as shown.

```
use anyhow::Result;
<Snip>
    Ok(http::Response::builder()
        .status(200)
        .header("content-type", "text/plain")
        .body("Docker loves Wasm")?)   <<---- Change
}
```

Compile it to Wasm.

```
$ spin build
Building component with `cargo build --target wasm32-wasi --release`
<Snip>
Finished building all Spin components
```

Create a new file called **Dockerfile** in the same directory with the following three lines.

```
FROM scratch
COPY /target/wasm32-wasi/release/hello_world.wasm .
COPY spin.toml .
```

Edit the `spin.toml` file and remove the leading path for the **source** line as shown. Don't forget to save your changes.

```
<Snip>
[component.hello-world]
source = "hello_world.wasm"        <<------ Change to this
<Snip>
```

Containerize the Wasm app with the following command. Use your own Docker username instead of mine.

```
$ docker build \
  --platform wasi/wasm \
  --provenance=false \
  -t nigelpoulton/gsd-book:wasm .
```

List the image.

```
$ docker images
REPOSITORY              TAG    IMAGE ID       CREATED       SIZE
nigelpoulton/gsd-book   wasm   1fb247c79452   8 secs ago    556kB
```

Push it to Docker Hub. Be sure to substitute your image name.

```
$ docker push nigelpoulton/gsd-book:wasm
```

Deploy as a Wasm container.

```
$ docker run -d --name wasm-ctr \
  --runtime=io.containerd.spin.v1 \
  --platform=wasi/wasm \
  -p 5556:80 \
  nigelpoulton/gsd-book:wasm /
```

Connect a browser to `http://localhost:5556/hello` to see the app.

Delete the container and image. Remember to change the image name to match yours.

```
$ docker rm wasm-ctr -f

$ docker rmi nigelpoulton/gsd-book:wasm
```

Terminology

This glossary defines some of the most common Docker and container-related terms used in the book.

Ping me if you think I've missed anything important:

- gsd@nigelpoulton.com

As always, I know that some of you are passionate about technical term definitions. I'm OK with that, and I'm not saying my definitions are better than anyone else's — they're just here to be helpful.

Term	Definition (according to Nigel)
Container	A container is an isolated part of an OS designed to run a single application. To an application, a container looks exactly like a regular OS. Containers are smaller, faster, and more portable than virtual machines. We sometimes call them *Docker containers* or *OCI containers*
Compose	An open specification for defining, deploying, and managing multi-container microservices apps. Docker implements the Compose spec and provides the **docker compose** command to make it easy to work with Compose apps.
Containerize	The process of packaging an application and all dependencies into a container image.

Term	Definition (according to Nigel)
Docker	Platform that makes it easy to work with containerized apps. It allows you to build images, as well as run and manage standalone containers and multi-container apps.
Docker Desktop	Desktop application for Linux, Mac, and Windows that makes working with Docker easy. It has a slick UI and many advanced features, such as image management, vulnerability scanning, and Wasm support.
Docker Hub	High-performance OCI-compliant image registry. Docker Hub has over 57PB of storage and handles an average of 30K requests per second.
Docker, Inc.	US-based technology company making it easy for developers to build, ship, and run containerized applications. The company behind the Docker platform.
Dockerfile	Plain text file with instructions telling Docker how to package an app as an image.
Image	Archive containing a single application, all dependencies, and the metadata required to start the application as a container. We sometimes call them *OCI images*, *container images*, or *Docker images*.

Term	Definition (according to Nigel)
Microservices	Design pattern for modern applications. Application features are developed as their own small applications (microservices/containers) and communicate via APIs. They work together to form a useful application.
Open Container Initiative (OCI)	Lightweight governance body responsible for creating and maintaining standards for low-level container technologies such as images, runtimes, and registries. Docker creates OCI-compliant images, implements an OCI-compliant runtime, and Docker Hub is an OCI-compliant registry.
Push	Upload an image to a registry.
Pull	Download an image from a registry.
Registry	Central place for storing and retrieving images. We sometimes call them *OCI registries*.
Spin	Framework that makes it easy to build, deploy, and run Wasm apps. Docker Desktop ships with the **spin** runtime. Created by Fermyon Technologies, Inc.
Wasm	See WebAssembly.

Term	Definition (according to Nigel)
WebAssembly	Also known as Wasm. New virtual machine architecture that is smaller, faster, more portable, and more secure than traditional containers. Wasm apps run anywhere with a Wasm runtime.

Index

L

M

N

O

P

R

S

W

More from the author

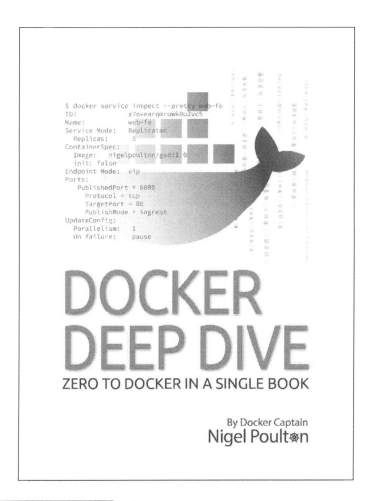

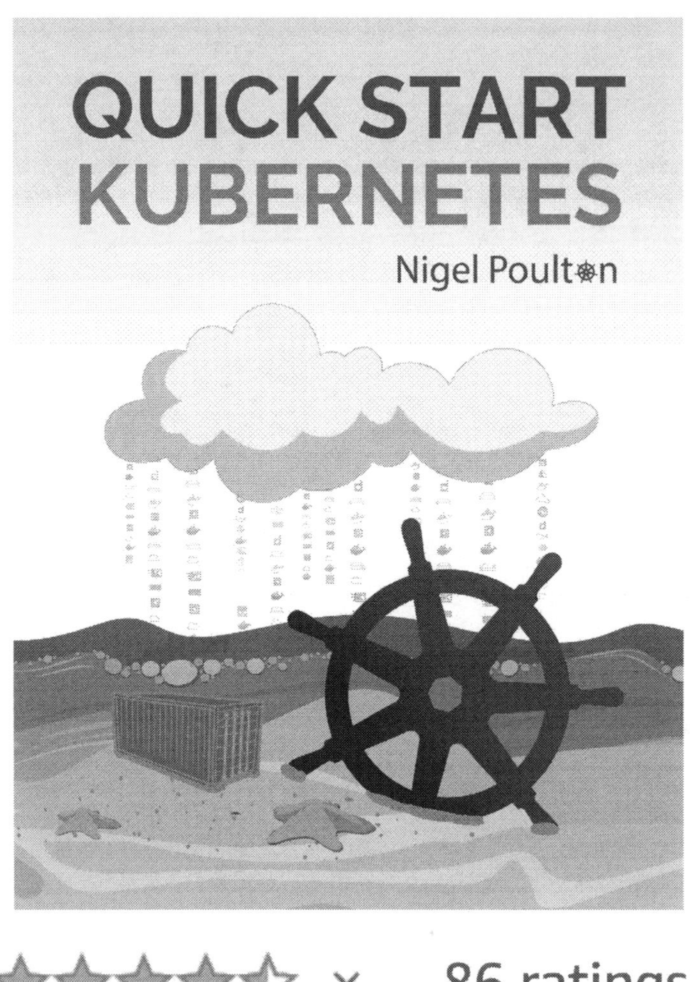

Quick Start Kubernetes is the best, and fastest way to get started Kubernetes. Whether you're a developer, sysadmin, architect, management, or even sales, the easy-to-follow examples in this book will get you up-to-speed in no time.
It's like this book, just for Kubernetes.

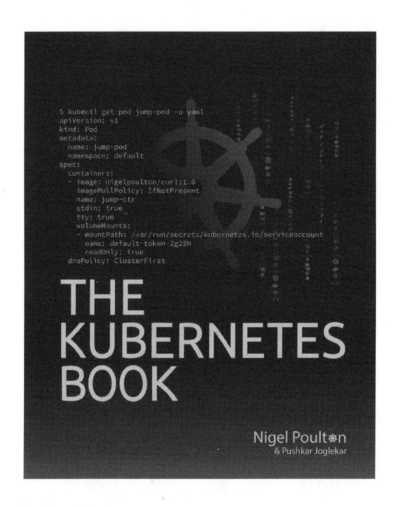

Show some love!

Enjoyed the book!

Head over to Amazon and give it some stars and a review.

Writing books is incredibly hard, and I spent many late nights and early mornings making this book as amazing as possible for you. Taking a couple of minutes to leave a review would be great.
Thanks!

Made in the USA
Las Vegas, NV
20 April 2024

88920851R00063